AS/A-LEVEL YEAR 1

STUDENT GUIDE

EDEXCEL

Economics A

Theme 2

The UK economy: performance and policies

PHILIP ALLAN FOR
HODDER
EDUCATION
AN HACHETTE UK COMPANY

Philip Allan, an imprint of Hodder Education, an Hachette UK company, Blenheim Court, George Street, Banbury, Oxfordshire OX16 5BH

Orders

Bookpoint Ltd, 130 Milton Park, Abingdon, Oxfordshire OX14 4SB

tel: 01235 827827

fax: 01235 400401

e-mail: education@bookpoint.co.uk

Lines are open 9.00 a.m.–5.00 p.m., Monday to Saturday, with a 24-hour message answering service. You can also order through the Hodder Education website: www.hoddereducation.co.uk

© Rachel Cole 2015

ISBN 978-1-4718-4408-9

First printed 2015

Impression number 10 9 8 7 6

Year 2022 2021 2020 2019 2018

This Guide has been written specifically to support students preparing for the Edexcel AS and A level Economics (Theme 2) examinations. The content has been neither approved nor endorsed by Edexcel and remains the sole responsibility of the author.

Typeset by Integra Software Services Pvt. Ltd., Pondicherry, India

Cover photo: ortodoxfoto/Fotolia

Printed in Dubai

Hachette UK's policy is to use papers that are natural, renewable and recyclable products and made from wood grown in sustainable forests. The logging and manufacturing processes are expected to conform to the environmental regulations of the country of origin.

Contents

Content Guidance

Questions & Answers

■ Getting the most from this book

Exam tips

Advice on key points in the text to help you learn and recall content, avoid pitfalls, and polish your exam technique in order to boost your grade.

Knowledge check

Rapid-fire questions throughout the Content Guidance section to check your understanding.

Knowledge check answers

1 Turn to the back of the book for the Knowledge check answers.

Summaries

■ Each core topic is rounded off by a bullet-list summary for quick-check reference of what you need to know.

Exam-style questions

Commentary on the questions

Tips on what you need to do to gain full marks, indicated by the icon **e**

Sample student answers

Practise the questions, then look at the student answers that follow.

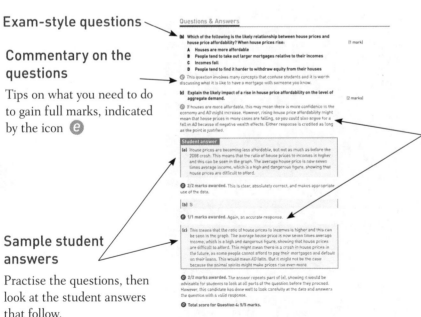

Commentary on sample student answers

Find out how many marks each answer would be awarded in the exam and then read the comments (preceded by the icon **e**) following each student answer. Annotations that link back to points made in the student answers show exactly how and where marks are gained or lost.

■About this book

The aim of this guide is to help you prepare for the Edexcel AS and A level Economics Paper 2 examinations. It includes all of the topics required for the AS exam Paper 2 'The UK economy: performance and policies' (code 8EC0/02) and some of the topics for the A level exam Paper 2 'The national and global economy' (code 9EC0/02). The concepts and models covered in this guide also directly feed into the synoptic A level exam Paper 3 'Microeconomics and macroeconomics' (code 9EC0/03).

This guide should be used as a supplement for a taught course along with textbooks and other materials recommended by your teacher. There are two sections:

- The **Content Guidance** section summarises the specification content of Theme 2 required for both the AS and the A level economics syllabus. Theme 2 'The UK economy: performance and policies' is based on the aggregate demand and supply model which underpins the whole syllabus. Theme 2's content comprises five main topics and a summary of key points is provided during and at the end of each one in this guide.
- The **Questions & Answers** section provides guidance on how to answer both the AS exam Paper 2 and the A level exam Paper 2. It includes multiple-choice and short-answer questions, data response questions and extended open-response questions. It also includes student answers and a commentary on how to improve performance.

Specification

The AS Economics specification is structured into two themes and consists of two exam papers, one on each theme. The first theme is 'Introduction to markets and market failure', which corresponds with exam Paper 1 of the same name. The second theme is 'The UK economy: performance and policies', which corresponds with exam Paper 2 of the same name. Note that this guide prepares students for exam Paper 2.

The A level Economics specification is structured into four themes and consists of three exam papers. In addition to the two AS themes, there is Theme 3 'Business behaviour and the labour market' and Theme 4 'A global perspective'.

The A level exam Paper 2 'The national and global economy' tests models and concepts from Themes 2 and 4. Consequently, it is important to study both themes ('The UK economy: performance and policies and 'A global perspective') in preparation for taking exam Paper 2.

Exam format

The AS exam Paper 2 'The UK economy: performance and policies' has two sections. Section A comprises five compulsory multiple-choice and short-answer questions; section B comprises one data-response question broken down into a number of parts, the last being an open-response question which offers students a choice from two. The time allowed for the examination is 1 hour and 30 minutes.

The A level exam Paper 2 'The national and global economy' has three sections. Section A comprises five compulsory multiple-choice and short-answer questions; section B comprises one compulsory data-response question broken down into a number of parts; section C comprises one extended open-response question which offers students a choice from two. The time allowed for the examination is 2 hours.

Note that the A level exam Paper 2 requires students to answer questions from Theme 2 'The UK economy: performance and policies' and Theme 4 'A global perspective'. Students are required to learn the models and concepts from both themes in preparation for the exam. You are therefore advised to obtain the accompanying student guide in this series, 'A global perspective', which provides further guidance on the content and exam questions for Theme 4.

Content Guidance

■ Measures of economic performance

Economic growth

GDP as a measure of economic growth

Gross domestic product (GDP) is the measure of output of goods and services in a country in a year. It is given as a level of output, in the local currency. On its own it is almost meaningless: we need to know how many people there are, what the currency is worth in terms of its spending power in the local economy and what the changes have been since the previous measure.

There are two meanings of the term *economic growth*: *actual economic growth* is an increase in real incomes or gross domestic product (GDP); *potential economic growth* is an increase in the productive capacity in a country. This might be because the labour supply has increased, there has been investment or productivity has increased. It can be used to show how an economy is performing relative to its output capacity. Differences between actual and potential growth are known as the *output gap*. Although it is a useful measure, potential economic growth is hard to record accurately. (See shifts in *AD* and *AS* on pp. 24–33 and output gaps on pp. 40–42.)

GDP is the sum of all goods and services produced in a country in a year. It is also the sum of all incomes earned in a country in a year and the sum of all expenditure in a year. GDP does not include earnings by its residents while outside the country. Consider it as a circular flow of income where for everything that is earned, something must be produced and something must be spent. The government measures all three flows — goods, income and expenditure — which should, in theory, amount to the same figure (currently around £1.4 trillion in the UK). However, in practice, errors and omissions mean that there are some discrepancies.

Increases in GDP are therefore a sign that a country is experiencing increasing incomes, output and spending. On the face of it, this is a good thing because people can have more goods and services, implying that they have a better standard of living. However, there are many reasons why this might not be the case. If someone earns more, it may be that they work longer hours and have more work pressures, or that they have a higher cost of living such as increased mortgage payments. Pollution is likely to increase as they travel greater distances and there are a whole range of social costs that may be incurred.

Knowledge check 1

Why is economic growth not the same as GDP?

Exam tip

The rate of increase in GDP in real terms is known as actual economic growth. It means there is more spending, higher incomes and higher output in the economy.

Furthermore, for GDP to have any significance in terms of standards of living, figures must be given per head (*per capita*). If a country's income increases by 10% but the population increases by 20%, people are actually worse off per head.

> **Exam tip**
>
> Standards of living include factors besides economic growth, although economic growth has a part to play in increasing living standards if the increased incomes are spread out across the economy.

Distinction between various terms

If economic growth is measured using national income, the value is meaningless unless the figures are given in **real values** rather than **nominal values**. Real values have been adjusted to remove the effects of inflation, whereas nominal values are the current incomes that you would see if they were unadjusted.

> **Exam tip**
>
> Real values have the effects of inflation removed. If inflation is 2% and your wage rise is 2%, your real wages have not risen at all.

Another important distinction required when measuring economic growth is to look at *values* rather than *volumes*. Firms might achieve higher sales figures because they sell more in volume or number of products, but if those sales are worth less per unit then they are not seeing an increase in the value of their output. As an example, consider Germany and China. Germany is the biggest exporter in the world by value, whereas China exports much more in terms of volume of goods.

Other national income measures

Other measures of output are increasingly used. *Gross national product* (GNP) is the total market value of all goods and services produced by domestic residents (GDP) plus income that residents have received from abroad, minus income claimed by non-residents. GNP may be much less than GDP if much of the income from a country's production flows to foreign people or firms. However, if the people or firms of a country hold large amounts of the stocks and bonds of firms or governments of other countries, and receive income from them, GNP may be greater than GDP.

Gross national income (GNI) is an augmented version of GDP. It is GDP plus income paid into the country by other countries for such things as interest and dividends. GNI is defined as the sum of value added by all producers who are residents in a nation, plus any product taxes (minus subsidies) not included in output, plus income received from abroad such as employee compensation and property income. GNI measures income received by a country both domestically and from overseas.

Both GNP and GNI measure output from the citizens and companies of a particular nation, regardless of whether they are located within its boundaries or overseas.

> **Exam tip**
>
> GDP is best measured in real terms, per capita.

Real values Values that have been adjusted to remove the effects of inflation. The effects are removed using an index number that represents the changes in prices and the results are called *constant values*.

Nominal values Values that are measured in money terms. Nominal figures are the unadjusted, current values.

> **Knowledge check 2**
>
> What is the difference between constant (real) prices GDP and current (nominal) GDP?

Comparison of rates of growth between countries and over time

An increase in GDP of 10% in one country does not mean that the country is doing better than a country with an increase of 5%. Similarly, changes over time have a different meaning: for example, increases in GDP in Japan in the 1960s were 10% a year compared to only 4% a year in the 1980s, but the 1980s figure was based on a much larger economy. An evaluation of growth figures depends on:

- how well-off the country is in the first place
- how much of the output is self-consumed, so does not appear as GDP
- methods of calculation and reliability of data
- relative exchange rates — do they represent the purchasing power of the local currency?
- type of spending by government — is money spent on warfare or on quality of life issues such as education and health?

> **Knowledge check 3**
>
> What is the difference between GNP and GNI? Which measure is more useful for a country, such as Greece, that has been borrowing heavily from another country?

Purchasing power parities (PPPs)

Purchasing power parities (PPPs) are when values are expressed in accordance with the amount that the currency will buy in the local economy. 'At value for GDP at PPPs' means that the exchange rate used is the one where the same basket of goods in the country could be bought in the USA at this rate of currency exchange. This makes international comparisons much more helpful because where the cost of living is high it would be expected that the PPP value of the GDP would be lower.

Limitations of using GDP to compare living standards between countries and over time

Let's say that economic growth is 10% in China, 6% in Bangladesh and around 2% in the UK. These figures may mask several differences not accounted for in GDP statistics:

- *Subsistence, barter and the hidden economy.* If farmers consume their own output, if goods are traded without the price system (e.g. by barter) or if goods are paid for without being declared for tax purposes, national income will not reflect the true standard of living. Estimates of the size of the hidden economy are UK 7%, Italy 30%, Russia 50% and sub-Saharan Africa up to 60%.
- *The informal economy.* Some output is not recorded because it is not bought or sold, but it is still output. For example, if a volunteer runs a charity shop this is output of a service, but there is no corresponding income. If someone grows their own potatoes this is output just as if they had bought them, but the home-grown ones are not recorded.
- *Currency values.* When trying to compare countries, there is a difficulty in knowing whether to use the official value of a currency (the exchange rate) or the purchasing power of that currency.
- *Income distribution.* When comparing countries' income per head, some sense of the income distribution should also be taken into account. In some cases, a large proportion of income is earned by a very few, which makes the mean income much higher than the income enjoyed by the ordinary person. In this way, the general standard of living in a country can appear higher than it really is for most people.

- *Size of the public sector.* If much of the spending in the economy is by government, it might or might not improve welfare for the population. The public sector is the part of the economy controlled by the government. It is around 50% of the UK economy, but in developing countries it is usually significantly less than 20%.
- *Consumer and capital spending.* Spending on investment goods might mean standard of living increases in the future, but at the expense of living standards today. It is better to take account of future growth patterns rather than simply considering today's income, and stark economic growth figures should be broken down to look at the investment element.
- *Quality issues.* Spending on schools might be high, for example, but how can we measure quality? Are improving results enough to prove that living standards are rising?

These limitations mean that comparisons of living standards are likely to be inaccurate if they are based solely on GDP. However, real income growth per head is a good guide to actual growth if these other factors are taken into account.

National happiness

Another response to the limitations of using GDP is to take into account other measures of living standards apart from material goods and trying to measure the quality of life. One example is to measure national happiness, rather than just focusing on monetary variables. The Gross National Happiness (GNH) Index has been designed in an attempt to define an indicator and concept that measures quality of life in more holistic and psychological terms than only using GDP. However, the index has only officially been used in Bhutan. In the UK, the ONS measures national wellbeing (tinyurl.com/d7ocy3k).

Within the area of happiness economics, some people refer to the *Easterlin paradox*, which is the idea that happiness rises with average incomes, but only up to a point. Beyond this, the marginal gains in happiness fall, perhaps because people care about relative as well as absolute incomes. One conclusion we may draw from this is that government policy should not be aimed at only economic growth. There are other aims such as reducing income inequality or external costs, which might have far greater impact on standards of living than having more money.

> **Exam tip**
>
> Make sure you know the limitations of measuring GDP and the possible solutions to them.

> **Knowledge check 4**
>
> Bhutan is ranked top of the GNH Index, but it has one of the lowest GDPs per capita in the world. How is this apparent paradox explained?

> **Knowledge check 5**
>
> Why do developing countries tend to have higher economic growth rates than developed countries?

Links and common themes

- The issues of the external costs of increased economic growth are discussed in Theme 1. You do not need to know the externalities diagram for Theme 2, but the concept of spillover effects is the same.
- Both an increase in aggregate demand and an increase in aggregate supply may increase the rate of growth in an economy, but not always. (See the section on economic growth, pp. 38–44.)
- Growth can increase living standards, but policies to increase growth might worsen the environment or widen income gaps. (See the section on macroeconomic policy conflicts, pp. 54–56.)
- Growth is often thought of as a necessary but not sufficient condition to relieve poverty in developing countries. This is a topic you are likely to discuss in Theme 4.

Inflation

Inflation, deflation and disinflation

Inflation is a sustained rise in the general price level. The general price level is measured using an index such as the *consumer prices index* (CPI). The reason for using an index is that percentage changes can be shown easily, making effective comparisons possible.

Deflation is a fall in the general price level. It is a problem for people with debts, because the real payments (having adjusted for lower prices) will become larger. Deflation is a problem because it stops any firm wanting to invest in a country from abroad as the value of output is likely to fall relative to the initial costs and deflation is likely to cause aggregate demand to fall. Why buy an expensive consumer item when you know prices are going to come down?

Disinflation occurs when prices rise more slowly than they have done in the past. For example, inflation might fall from 3% to 2%, meaning that prices are rising but less quickly than they were. Disinflation can be a sign that inflation is coming under control, but on the worrying side it can mean that investment and confidence are low in the economy, and deflation might occur in the near term.

Calculating the rate of inflation using the CPI

Two surveys need to be undertaken to calculate inflation (if the figure is negative then this is deflation, but the process of calculation is the same). The first survey on expenditure involves the collection of information about what people buy, currently known as the Office of National Statistics (ONS) Living Costs and Food Survey (LCF). This is a survey carried out by the ONS that involves collecting information from a sample of nearly 7,000 households in the UK using self-reported diaries of all purchases, including food eaten out. The proportion of income spent on each item is used to ascertain weighting. For example, if 10% is spent on food, then 10% of the weighting is assigned to food. This is an annual survey that is used to determine the contents of a virtual 'basket' of goods and services that households spend their money on, and the proportion spent on each.

The second survey is of prices. The price survey is undertaken by civil servants who collect data once a month about changes in the price of the 650 most commonly used goods and services in a variety of retail outlets. Because similar items can be bought in high and low cost shops, a selection of prices is gathered for each item, with 120,000 prices gathered in all. The price changes are multiplied by the weights to give a price index. You can measure inflation from this by calculating the percentage change in this index over consecutive years.

The limitations of the CPI

The UK government's target for CPI inflation is 2% and there is a tolerance of one percentage point either way. As a brief way of writing this we say 2% (± 1%), but of course the target is 2% and the plus or minus 1% merely gives the range that is deemed acceptable. This means that small price rises are acceptable to the UK government. If prices rise by more than 3% they become a concern, but if they begin to rise by less than 1%, or even fall, then risks of deflation and even a recession might arise.

Inflation A general and sustained increase in prices, measured by a change in a weighted index of prices such as the CPI.

Knowledge check 6

Why is an index used to measure inflation?

Deflation A fall in the general level of prices, i.e. negative inflation.

Disinflation A fall in the rate of inflation, i.e. prices are rising more slowly.

Exam tip

The CPI measures price levels, not the level of inflation — unless you are given 'CPI inflation', which means inflation as measured using the CPI.

Knowledge check 7

Why are there two surveys for the CPI?

Another problem with the CPI measure is that it does not include housing costs such as mortgage interest repayments or rent. Monthly mortgage payments often form a large part of a household's spending and are certainly a cost of living for almost 10 million households in the UK, with average mortgage payments costing 15–20% of income. Therefore, if the CPI rises by only 2% and inflation seems to be under control, a rise in interest rates means that many households will nevertheless be experiencing the effect of higher mortgage payments, i.e. their cost of living rises. In this case, a wage rise linked to CPI excludes a significant change in living costs.

Knowledge check 8

Is it true to say that measures such as the CPI are described as 'excluding mortgages'?

There are several other issues with the CPI as a measure of the rate of inflation:

- The CPI measures the cost of living only for an average household. The top and bottom 4% income brackets are not included, and nor are pensioners.
- There are sampling problems: only 57% of households respond to the survey, and when they do respond they might not give accurate information about recent spending of various members within the household.
- The list of 650 items is changed only once a year, but tastes and fashions change more quickly than this. In addition, the list does not reflect the fact that changes in retail outlets' promotions such as 'buy one, get one free' temporarily change people's spending habits.
- For people with atypical spending patterns, such as vegetarians and non-drivers, the CPI is unrepresentative. For example, those who often buy rail tickets may experience a personal inflation well above 2% with recent rises in train fares.
- When the quality of goods changes, the measure breaks down because it is not comparing like with like. For example, if someone bought a more expensive mobile phone this year than last year, the price change might not be the result of inflation but because they wanted an upgrade.

The RPI as an alternative measure

For many people, wage increases are linked to the rate of inflation and, if the CPI measure is used, wage increases will fail to take into account a large part of household expenditure in the form of housing costs. A more appropriate measure for wage increases is the **retail price index (RPI)**. This is more inclusive than the CPI in that it includes housing costs, but it is not as reliable for international comparisons and the statistical method of basing the data is also unique to the UK. Moreover, because the RPI includes the cost of mortgage interest repayments and these will rise when interest rates are raised, any interest rate rise implemented to tackle inflation will have a one-off effect of making inflation appear worse, which makes the policy-makers look incompetent.

Knowledge check 9

Why does the government like to exclude housing costs in the main measure of inflation?

Retail price index (RPI) An index used to measure inflation that includes housing costs such as mortgage interest repayments.

Knowledge check 10

Although you may be able to explain the distinction between CPI and RPI inflation measures, can you explain how one measure can rise while the other falls, or why they might come closer together or move further apart?

Useful exercises

Carry out an online search for 'Economy tracker BBC' to find up-to-date figures on inflation, GDP, jobs, interest rates and house prices.

The causes of inflation

In order to understand how monetary policy works, it is important to consider the causes of inflation. In terms of *AD/AS* analysis, inflation can be shown as a shift to the right in *AD* or a shift to the left in *AS*. A shift to the right in *AD* is often called **demand-pull inflation** and it occurs whenever *AD* shifts to the right, usually exacerbated by multiplier effects. A shift to the left in *AS* is known as **cost-push inflation** and occurs whenever costs of production increase in an economy. These might be for short-term reasons, such as a fall in the exchange rate making imports more expensive, or for longer-term reasons, such as higher corporation taxes.

However, according to monetarists such as Milton Friedman, inflation is 'always and everywhere a monetary phenomenon' (*Monetary History of the United States 1867–1960*, 1963). That is, monetarists believe that inflation is caused by increases in the **money supply** above the rate of the increase in the real output in the economy. Inflation can be controlled by controlling the money supply, either directly or more effectively perhaps through the rate of interest.

The effects of inflation

The costs of inflation include problems for consumers, firms, the government and workers, but there are also some benefits.

For consumers

- *The real value of savings falls as prices rise.* People of working age are already significantly under-saving in the UK and inflation makes saving even less attractive.
- *The purchasing power of those on fixed incomes falls as prices rise.* For example, pensioners relying on annuities for their main living expenditures will find their standards of living decline when there is inflation.
- *Those with high levels of personal debt benefit from inflation, as the real value of the debt falls.* The value of a mortgage loan relative to income is likely to fall when the general level of prices rise.

For firms

- *Loss of international competitiveness.* Exports become relatively expensive and imports relatively cheap. The balance of payments is likely to worsen.

Exam tip

Don't confuse price levels (e.g. CPI) with rates of inflation. Increases in CPI are inflation. The rate of inflation may fall even when price levels are still rising. If inflation is above zero but falling, the price level is rising at a slower rate.

Knowledge check 11

How is inflation measured? (Clue: Many students waste a lot of time by saying what inflation is. Instead start with the two surveys and remember to refer to weights in your answer.)

Demand-pull inflation An increase in the general level of prices caused by increased consumption, investment, government spending or net exports.

Cost-push inflation An increase in the general level of prices caused by increased production costs such as a rise in wages or a fall in the exchange rate (imports expensive).

Money supply The amount of spending power in an economy. It includes cash and bank deposits. Monetarists believe that an increase in the money supply has a direct relationship with inflation.

- *Increased uncertainty.* If firms think that costs are rising and fear increases in interest rates, they might curb investment.
- *Investment from abroad might decrease.* Inflation erodes the value of money, so why buy into a currency that is falling in value?
- *Increased prices might be a sign that firms can make more profits.* In contrast to the above point about uncertainty, it might mean that investment is encouraged.
- *A little inflation means that real wage differentials can be changed without actually cutting wages in nominal terms.* The argument is that people will accept wage rises below the rate of inflation but will never accept wage cuts.

For the government

- *Redistribution of income.* Those on fixed incomes will find incomes fall in real terms. Those with index-linked incomes will not lose out unless they are linked to a fairly unrepresentative measure such as the CPI.
- *Inflation reduces the real interest rate, so the cost of borrowing falls.* The UK government has public debt approaching £1.5 trillion, but the real value of the debt falls when there is inflation.
- *A little inflation provides a cushion against the perils of deflation.* When prices are falling, the economy can run into a vicious circle of underinvestment and reduced spending.

For workers

- *Inflation might mean that some workers expect high wages but firms do not feel confident about paying higher costs.* This is particularly true if firms cannot pass on the higher costs in terms of higher prices. So some workers find it hard to get work, especially if there is uncertainty and fears that the interest rate might be raised.
- *According to some economists, there is a trade-off between wage inflation and unemployment (the short-run Phillips curve).* This means that if there is high wage inflation, it is easier for people to find work because firms are raising wages only because they cannot choose other workers at lower wages.

Useful exercises

- Carry out an online search for 'Personal inflation calculator' to find the online assessment on the BBC News Business website. Complete the boxes to calculate your own rate of inflation. Next, imagine you are a pensioner living alone on a small income and do the same. Do you think incomes for students and pensioners should be linked to a measure of inflation more reflective of both of your spending patterns?
- Visit the Bank of England website at www.bankofengland.co.uk to see the current rate of inflation, the current rate of interest and recent inflation reports. Alternatively, if you live near London, visit the Bank of England museum in Threadneedle Street. Entry is free.

Knowledge check 12

What causes inflation?

Exam tip

In the context of the UK economy, menu costs, shoe leather costs and the dangers of entering a wage-price spiral tend to be insignificant and not worth researching for your exam.

Knowledge check 13

What is the ideal rate of inflation for an economy?

Employment and unemployment

The *level of employment* is the number of people in work, whereas the *rate of employment* is the proportion of people in work relative to the size of the **workforce**. The workforce consists of those people who are at work or those of working age who are willing and able to work (i.e. the employed *and the unemployed*).

The unemployed are people who are willing and available to work, but are not currently employed. The *level of unemployment* is the number of people out of work, and the *rate of unemployment* gives this figure as a proportion of the workforce.

Measures of unemployment

There are two main ways of measuring unemployment: the claimant count and the UK Labour Force Survey.

The claimant count

The **claimant count** is a measure of unemployment that records the number of people who are claiming Jobseeker's Allowance (JSA) or other benefits principally for the reason of being unemployed such as Universal Credit. There is some stigma attached to claiming benefits, so not everyone who is eligible to claim does so, and many are not eligible because the criteria for eligibility are tight. For example, if you have resigned from your previous job within the last 6 months or refused three jobs that you have been offered, you cannot claim.

In order to gain the full benefit of around £73 a week, you need to have made a certain number of National Insurance (NI) contributions by working in the past. You also have to prove, in an interview at the Jobcentre every 2 weeks, that you are looking for work ('signing on'). Under the rules of the New Deal, you might be denied benefits unless you actively involve yourself in training or work placements. After 6 months of claiming JSA you will be means-tested, and claims are substantially reduced if you have a partner who earns an income or if you have savings above £6,000; payments are stopped altogether if you have more than £16,000. You must be over 18 and below retirement age (although the rate of JSA is significantly lower for those aged 18–25 than for those over 25). If you are unable to work or are working in a voluntary capacity for more than 16 hours a week, you cannot claim.

Therefore, the claimant count does not present the full picture of unemployment. However, it is quick and cheap to obtain these data (they are a by-product of the process of administering benefits) and a useful measure of hardship — after all, you are not likely to claim JSA if you don't need the money between jobs.

The International Labour Organization (ILO) and the UK Labour Force Survey

The International Labour Organization uses the **Labour Force Survey**, which is now the official measure used in the UK. It is a legal requirement for every EU country to conduct this survey and each country must use the same methods. This involves a face-to-face interview followed by a quarterly telephone survey of 80,000 households, asking several questions including whether anyone in the household has been out of work for 4 weeks and is ready to start in the next 2 weeks. The questions relate to anyone over the age of 16, and it is therefore a more inclusive survey than the

Workforce A measure of people of working age who are willing and able to work.

Knowledge check 14

What is the difference between the employment rate and the employment level?

Claimant count A measure of unemployment using the number of claimants of JSA.

Knowledge check 15

Is the claimant count the measure of those eligible to receive JSA or the number receiving it?

Labour Force Survey A measure of unemployment of those out of work in the last 4 weeks and ready to start in the next 2 weeks.

claimant count. However, the survey data are 6 weeks out of date by the time they are published, which happens (by sampling) every month.

The distinction between unemployment and underemployment

Many people have some work but not enough hours to give them the pay they would like, or are in jobs that do not pay as much as they expect given their qualifications. For example, a classically trained musician might get some work playing in concerts at the weekends but not every day of the week, and he might have to fill the time working as a cleaner to make up his income. The idea of **underemployment** became particularly important in the wake of the 2008 global financial crisis. The number of underemployed workers was fairly stable over the period before the onset of the economic downturn in 2008, but between 2008 and 2012 it increased by up to 50%.

This means that the figures for **unemployment** may be misleading (Figure 1). It looks as if unemployment did not rise post-2008 as much as it did after previous recessions in the UK. But if underemployment is taken into account, it is clear that the jobs market has experienced a significant downfall.

Knowledge check 16

At the current time the claimant count is under 1 million while the ILO method records over 2 million. What factors might account for this dramatic two-fold difference?

Underemployment
A situation in which a worker is employed but wants to work more hours.

Unemployment
A situation in which someone is willing and available to work, but is not currently employed.

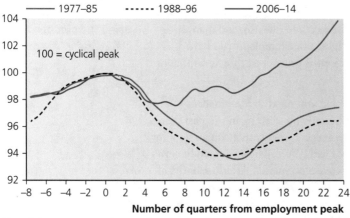

Note: Private sector employment has risen by about 2.1m (9.1%) since the end of 2009

Figure 1 Index of employment over three time periods in the UK

Source: ONS, Labour Force Survey

Changes in the rates of employment, unemployment and inactivity

Employment is affected by the following factors:

- *The school or compulsory training leaving age.* This will rise to 18 in summer 2015, which will have the effect of making the workforce smaller because anyone in education or training is not counted as economically active. However, in the longer term, it is likely to make school leavers more employable.
- *Number of school leavers entering higher or further education.* Although over 40% of students now carry on in education after 18 in the UK, this is likely to fall now that many students have to pay over £9,000 a year in university fees.
- *Level of net migration.* Net migration is the difference between those coming into the country (*immigration*) and those leaving (*emigration*). Most immigrants into the UK come to study (37%), but the second-most common reason is related to work

(34%). Most UK immigrants come from the rest of the EU, and as EU inhabitants enjoy full rights to enter the UK for work. Immigration is likely to increase both employment and unemployment.

- *Availability of jobs.* There are likely to be higher levels of employment if there are more jobs available.
- *Level of taxes and benefits.* If taxes on income are high or out-of-work benefits are generous, there is a disincentive for people to work.

Over 20% of people of working age in the UK are neither employed nor unemployed. This is known as **inactivity** and comprises people who are of working age but are either not willing or not able to work. The bulk of inactive people are students in full-time (usually further) education and the many people looking after children or other dependants. There are also approximately 3 million people who are not able to work because of incapacity such as a health problem.

Inactivity A measure of people of working age who are either unwilling or unable to work.

The main problem with the measure of inactivity is that it can make the levels of unemployment look lower than they really are. Many students are looking for work to supplement their low incomes while studying, and many people are signed off work with a health impairment but would be keen to work if there were work that were possible. There are many carers of dependants (largely women) who are inactive who would like to work but cannot find employment that would cover the cost of childcare. These people do not feature on the unemployment figures but are a measure of hardship caused by the inability to find a suitable job.

The causes of unemployment

There are two very different views on the causes of unemployment. On one side, the Classical view, there are only unemployed people who are not able and willing to work at the going wage rate. In other words, if people would accept a lower wage they could find jobs. In this view, all unemployment is therefore just a short-term problem and the best solution is laissez faire — that is, leave the market to get on with it and eventually the problem of unemployment will go away. If people accept lower wages, the cost of living will fall as firms do not need to charge such high prices, so workers will find the lower wages are acceptable once they start working. For this reason, it is called **real wage unemployment** or real wage inflexibility because wages have been forced above the market-clearing wage. People who believe that this is the only cause of unemployment think that out-of-work benefits should be cut, trade unions should be curtailed and there should not be a minimum wage. Therefore, unemployed people will be forced to work.

Real wage unemployment A measure of people who are unwilling to work at the going wage rate. Classical economists believe that wages that are kept artificially above the market-clearing wage are a main cause of unemployment.

On the other hand, in the opposing Keynesian view, people can be unemployed even in the long run. This is because there is insufficient aggregate demand in the economy. If you agree that the economy can be in equilibrium but not everyone has a job, you are arguing that there is **demand-deficient unemployment**.

Keynes said that if people do not spend and save too much, there are multiplier effects in the economy, and less spending means there are fewer job opportunities. If people are losing jobs, there will be even less spending and so the vicious circle continues. Even if wages are cut, there will not be more people employed — in fact, lower wages will mean that there is even less spending, so even fewer people are needed in employment.

Demand-deficient unemployment Also known as cyclical unemployment, this is caused by a lack of aggregate demand in an economy such as during a recession.

Apart from saving too much, other reasons for demand-deficient unemployment include:

- a lack of business confidence
- an increase in the value of a currency
- slow rates of productivity growth relative to other countries
- external shocks such as oil price rises (oil is imported and demand is price inelastic, so if prices rise there will be less spending in the UK)
- increased use of imports from low wage economies

Keynesians believe that demand-deficient unemployment can at certain times be a main cause of unemployment, and a fiscal or monetary stimulus may be needed to reduce this.

Another argument for employment problems that are not linked solely to an unwillingness of labour to work at the going rate is that the economy is undergoing structural change and therefore different types of labour are required. The skill set of those, for example, who are trained in manufacturing will not have much value in a business based in the service sector. Clearly, over time, as fewer people are trained for manufacturing and more for services, this kind of structural unemployment will disappear. However, as Keynes said, 'in the long run we are all dead', so in the view of many there ought to be proactive policies put in place to deal with both demand-deficient and structural kinds of unemployment.

There will always be frictional unemployment — people who are moving from one job to another — but this kind of unemployment is a sign of a healthy, flexible labour market with people willing to change jobs in order to improve their prospects. Another type that is problematic in some countries is seasonal unemployment, which measures people who can find work for some of the year, such as ski instructors or vegetable pickers, but have trouble finding work at other times of the year. This type of unemployment should be addressed by developing the mobility of labour: an improvement in skills means that these workers could find other work in other fields and geographical mobility might mean they could work in other countries as peak demand for agricultural workers changes according to climate.

The significance of migration and skills for employment and unemployment

Migration is a term that looks at both immigration (people moving into a country) and emigration (people moving out of a country). Net migration is immigration minus emigration. Migration may occur because people are looking for work or better paid work, or because they do not agree with the way in which they are being taxed. There are also many social reasons for migration such as to study abroad, as a result of social and political problems in the original country, to accompany family members or to follow a different lifestyle.

The implications of immigration for employment and unemployment depend largely on the reasons for the migration. If immigrants come into a country to fill vacancies, immigration leads to an increase in employment. However, if immigrants are looking for work and either do not find it or displace other people from work, employment many be unchanged and unemployment (surplus labour) might increase.

Structural unemployment
A measure of workers who lose jobs in a declining industry and do not have the skills to join other industries.

Frictional unemployment
A measure of people who are between jobs.

Seasonal unemployment
A measure of people who have jobs only at certain times of the year such as surfing instructors.

Knowledge check 17

Why does an increase in immigration tend to lead to an increase in employment and unemployment?

Knowledge check 18

If you add together employment and unemployment in the UK, you will reach a figure of around 80%. What are the other 20% doing?

The higher the level of skills in the labour force, the more flexible workers will be if there is a change in the requirements in the labour market. Employed people that are highly skilled are likely to be more able to move between jobs and stay in the market if there are shocks to the market. Unemployed people with high levels of skill and flexibility are unlikely to be unemployed for long.

Useful exercises

- Visit the Office for National Statistics website at www.ons.gov.uk and type in the phrase 'Labour Force Survey'. You will find a summary of how the survey operates and how the data is used in a short video guide.
- One explanation for the relative changes in the Labour Force Survey and the claimant count is the stage of the economic cycle. List two reasons why this might be so. Your reasons should bear in mind that the measures tend to get closer to each other in a deep recession as more people become eligible to claim JSA, and the hardship in the economy makes people more likely to claim if they can.
- Look up the JSA at www.gov.uk to find out all the eligibility criteria, current rates and more. You need to search the main site for 'Jobseeker's Allowance'.

Links and common themes

- When there are unemployed resources such as labour, the economy is operating inside its production possibility frontier (see Theme 1).
- Spare capacity is also a sign that there is an output gap, which is equivalent to the relatively elastic part of the aggregate supply curve, discussed on pp. 40–41.
- Inflation can redistribute incomes (e.g. from savers to borrowers) and some analysts believe that tolerating inflation means that lower levels of unemployment can be enjoyed. However, inflation makes a country less competitive if its inflation rate is higher than in the countries to which it exports. This could mean that a current account deficit develops or that the exchange rate falls, which is even more inflationary. These conflicts and compounding problems are discussed in the section on 'Conflicts and trade-offs between objectives and policies', pp. 54–56.

The effects of unemployment

The effects of unemployment to the economy include the following:

- *The cost to consumers*. People will have lower incomes and living standards will fall. However, there is a wider unseen cost as people out of work lose morale and there are repercussions for family members.
- *The cost to firms*. Firms will find that people spend less, so they will have to lower prices and make less profit. However, it may mean that people are more willing to stay in their jobs owing to fear of unemployment, so they may be willing to work harder.
- *The cost to workers*. Workers without work might find their skills become obsolete or at least out of date. For example, an office worker who has had some years out might be surprised to go back to work and find there are no faxes or scanners and technology has a whole new interface.

- *The cost to government.* As unemployment rises, the government has to pay more in jobseekers' benefits and will receive less in tax.
- *The cost to society as a whole.* Unemployed resources represent an opportunity cost. The economy could produce more without anything being given up. We could all have better standards of living. There are also people who think that unemployment causes crime, civil unrest and other social problems. However, you should be careful not to make speedy judgements: a lot of crime such as fraud is committed by people in work and social problems such as binge drinking cannot be easily sustained on the income from JSA.

Summary

- Employment is just over 30 million, meaning that in the UK almost one in every two people in the population works. The employment rate — the percentage of workers relative to the number of working age — is in the range of 70–80% in the UK.
- High levels of employment have benefits for the workers (higher incomes and the human capital factor — when you work, you gain or retain skills in industry), governments (lower payments of JSA, higher levels of tax receipts) and firms (higher levels of spending with multiplier effects). There are said to be improved social effects when people are busy.
- Unemployment in the UK reached 8% after the 2008–10 recession, although in many countries it was much higher.
- The remaining people of working age who are neither employed nor unemployed are either unwilling or unable to take on full-time work (students, houseworkers or people caring for family).

Balance of payments

Components of the balance of payments

The balance of payments is a record of payments between one country and the rest of the world. It comprises the current, financial and capital accounts. The most significant element of it is the current account.

Current account

The current account records trade in goods, trade in services, investment income and current transfers.

Trade in goods and services

Trade in goods measures the movement of tangible products across international borders. The UK is a large exporter of pharmaceuticals and cars, but a major importer of foodstuffs and, since 2005, a net importer of oil and gas. *Trade in services* measures movement of intangible output. The UK is a major exporter of banking and insurance services, but an importer of foreign holidays (because the British like to go abroad).

Investment income and current transfers

Investment income is a measure of interest, profit and dividends that are rewards for capital investments in another country. For example, if a British person buys shares in a US company, the shares do not appear on the current account, but any dividends appear as a positive figure on the UK current account. **Current transfers** refer to the movement of funds for which there is no corresponding trade in goods and services. Examples are taxes paid to the EU, payments to British military personnel working in another country and when economic migrants send some of their income back to their families in another country.

Current account deficits and surpluses

A country such as Germany, which exports a large number of high-value goods, has a **current account surplus**, meaning that more money flows in (for the purchase of German goods and services by foreigners) than flows out for imports. On the other hand, a country that enjoys a high living standard and a high level of confidence, and which is not as successful in export markets, is likely to be running a **current account deficit**, where outflows are greater than inflows. Examples are the USA, Spain and the UK.

> **Exam tip**
>
> There are four components of the current account of the balance of payments. If you disaggregate the figures (break them down into trade in goods, trade in services etc.), you will see that they are not all negative even if the overall balance is negative.

Financial and capital accounts

The main element of the balance of payments is the current account, but there are two other components that you should be aware of so that you don't confuse them with the current account. The first is the *financial account*, which records money flows for investment purposes: foreign direct investment (buying out assets and

> **Knowledge check 19**
>
> Are your holidays abroad an 'import'?

Investment income The reward for investments in other countries. It comprises interest, profit and dividends.

Current transfers The payment of money across international boundaries that has no corresponding output.

Current account surplus Where inflows on the current account of the balance of payments are greater than outflows.

Current account deficit Where outflows on the current account of the balance of payments are greater than inflows.

ownership of companies in other countries) and foreign portfolio investment ('hot money'), which is the speculative movement of money between countries as exchange rates and interest rates change.

The other account is the *capital account*, which puts the other two accounts in balance by recording the changes in net assets in each country, as well as errors and omissions.

Current account imbalances and other macroeconomic objectives

On its own, a balance of payments deficit on the current account is not a problem for an economy as long as it can be funded; it can be a sign that living standards are rising. It becomes a problem when reserves of foreign currencies begin to run low and we say that a country is not paying its way. It might mean that the currency falls in value, which is inflationary (imports become more expensive). It might be a sign that the country is becoming uncompetitive (costs are rising relative to trading partners), which can cause unemployment in the domestic economy and might in the long run mean that a painful re-adjustment, such as tax increases, is required to stop people overspending. Higher taxes and cuts in government spending might solve the deficit but are likely to cause a slowdown in economic growth.

> **Exam tip**
>
> One of the most common misunderstandings is the analysis of what happens to the current account of the balance of payments when the interest rate rises. This is only partially within the scope of this theme and will be discussed in detail in Theme 4, but it is important not to argue that '"hot money" enters the country and this improves the balance' because 'hot money' is not part of the current account. The best argument to pursue in Theme 2 is that, when the interest rate rises, the exchange rate usually rises also, so exports will become less competitive and imports more so.

> **Exam tip**
>
> If interest rates rise, the exchange rate is likely to rise. This makes exports relatively expensive, and imports relatively cheap, so it is likely to worsen the balance of payments in the long run.

Useful exercises

- Carry out an online search for 'UK balance of payments first release' with the current year to see a summary of the current account in recent years.
- The Pink Book (type 'Pink Book Balance of Payments' into a search engine) is more up to date and very detailed, but perhaps not so easy to interpret.

Links and common themes

- Many students find the current account the most mystifying of all the measures of economic performance. This is partly because Theme 2 is a holistic study and you need to know the rest of the theme before this part fully makes sense. Furthermore, it is just a partial look at international trade, which will be covered in more depth in Theme 4.

The interconnectedness of economies through international trade

International trade means that countries become interdependent, relying on each other both for income (through exports) and for resources and goods and services (through imports). This reliance means that the economies are increasingly connected and if one country or area suffers with weak demand this has a direct effect on other countries. For example, in recent times China has suffered slower growth as the recession in the southern European states continued.

Interconnectedness becomes a problem when deficits or surpluses on the current account become persistent. We call this a current account imbalance. The cause of a current account imbalance may be that a country is spending too much or that it is not producing anything that potential customers abroad want to buy. It may be because of the stage in the business cycle, which clearly may be different for different countries at different times, or the strength of the currency. For example, if sterling is strong against the dollar, the UK is likely to export less and import more because the price of UK exports rises relative to other products on the world market, and imports become relatively cheap in the UK.

Perhaps the most significant factor in the UK is the loss of competitiveness in the manufacturing sector owing to higher costs of factors of production in the UK relative to the Far East. It takes time for economies to adjust to changing comparative costs and during the adjustment process the UK is likely to face an ongoing deficit.

The costs of a current account imbalance become significant only when the deficit (or surplus) becomes unsustainable. *Sustainability* means that the needs of the present are met without compromising the ability of future generations to meet their own needs. Persistent deficits can make the value of a currency fall, so in some economies the government might try to buy up surplus currency in order to maintain its value. (This does not happen in the UK.)

A fall in the value of the currency may restore competitiveness, as it makes imports seem more expensive and exports relatively cheap on international markets. Persistent deficits see net incomes leave the country, which might mean demand in the domestic country is subdued. If you are a worker you might lose your job, but from the perspective of the Monetary Policy Committee of the Bank of England, subdued domestic demand might be a welcome development, preventing the onset of inflation.

Knowledge check 20

'America sneezes and the UK catches a cold.' Explain this statement using your understanding of the interconnectedness of economies through international trade.

Aggregate demand and supply

'Aggregate' means added together — the individual elements that were introduced in microeconomics are totalled in macroeconomics. Aggregate demand and supply analysis brings together the amount that consumers wish to consume and firms wish to produce at any price level.

Aggregate demand (AD) is the total planned expenditure on goods and services produced in the UK. **Aggregate supply (AS)** is the total planned output of goods and services. The equilibrium point where they meet determines the average price level and the equilibrium real output level. The price level can be measured by a price index such as the CPI and the output by real GDP.

The aggregate demand and supply model is probably the most useful tool for macroeconomists because it gives reasons for changes in the important macroeconomic variables: when price levels increase, this is inflation; when output increases, this is economic growth.

Aggregate demand (*AD*)

The characteristics of *AD*

Aggregate demand comprises consumption (*C*), investment (*I*), government expenditure (*G*) and exports (*X*) minus imports (*M*):

$$AD = C + I + G + (X - M)$$

When price levels fall, the level of *AD* expands along the *AD* curve; when price levels rise, aggregate demand contracts.

The *AD* curve is downward-sloping. This is not because 'people buy more things when they are cheaper' — the most common misunderstanding about the *AD* curve. There are three ways to explain the downward-sloping *AD* curve, any one of which is adequate for an answer in your exam:

- Lower prices in an economy mean increased international competitiveness, so there are more exports and fewer imports. In other words, net exports are higher at lower prices.
- The total amount of spending is approximately equal whether prices are high or low because people have approximately the same amount of money to spend, so the area under the curve is fairly constant. This is known as the *real balance effect*. If you plot a constant area, you will get a *rectangular hyperbola*.
- At higher price levels, interest rates are likely to be raised by the monetary authorities. This means that investment — a component of aggregate demand — falls and savings might increase.

Consumption (*C*)

Consumption, or spending by households on goods and services, is the main component of aggregate demand, comprising approximately 60%. It measures the amount that consumers wish to spend at various price levels rather than save. If you ignore tax and spending on imports, a person's income is either spent (*C*) or saved (*S*).

Aggregate demand (*AD*) The total planned expenditure on goods and services produced in the UK.

Aggregate supply (*AS*) The total planned output of goods and services in the UK.

Knowledge check 21

Is it true that *AD* increases because people spend more when everything is cheaper?

Exam tip

The *AD* curve does not shift when the price level changes. There will be a movement along the *AD*. For the *AD* to shift there must be a change in one of the components of *AD*, that is, *C*, *I*, *G*, *X* or *M*, as described in the next section.

The higher the income after tax (what we call *disposable income*), the more people are likely to spend, but they might spend at a slower rate as they earn more — i.e. people tend to save more as their incomes rise.

Apart from the level of income, there are other key factors that make people want to spend rather than save. The more people feel they need to save, the less they spend, and vice versa. One of the key determinants of consumption as opposed to saving is the confidence of the consumer, in terms of both job security and future income prospects. If consumers are feeling confident, they are more likely to make large purchases that they can pay for in the future. Another determinant is interest rates. Higher interest rates not only leave consumers with less spending money after housing costs, they also increase the cost of hire purchase. A third determinant is the housing market. When house prices accelerate upwards, home owners can extract more equity from their houses, as discussed in the section on 'Wealth effects' (see p. 34).

The high importance of consumption as a component of aggregate demand is evident in Figure 2. There is a correlation between consumer spending and the overall output of goods and services.

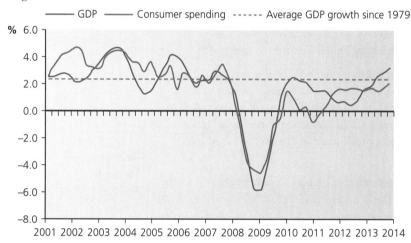

Note: Average revised GDP growth rate since mid-2009 = 1.8%

Figure 2 Percentage of annual change in GDP and consumer spending

Source: ONS

When house prices rise, does *AD* rise or fall?

Exam tip

Using Figure 2, select times when the consumer spending and GDP changes correlate less closely. Remember that real data never fully prove a theory, but they can provide evidence to support a pattern.

Knowledge check 22

Investment (*I*)

Gross and net investment

Investment is an increase in the capital stock. It means creating assets that will generate income in the future rather than in the immediate term. Investment forms around 10–15% of *AD*, but the figure depends on whether you are considering gross or net investment.

Gross investment is the total amount of investment before any account is taken of depreciation of assets. Capital loses value as it wears out or becomes less efficient. Many machines become totally redundant as new methods of production are invented and the investment in these machines does not have any long-term benefit on the economy.

Net investment takes account of the fall in value of capital assets. It is a more useful measure if you want to look at the productivity of an economy and its productive potential, although there are data collection questions on whether you can measure depreciation and different countries use different methods.

Influences on investment

Investors are driven by factors that are likely to determine future sales. Anything that improves confidence in future sales patterns is likely to lead to a rise in investment. The indicators of this are changes in the rate of economic growth, business expectations and confidence indicators (mainly carried out through surveys), what their main competitors are doing, government incentives and regulations.

There is an inverse relationship between interest rates and the level of investment that firms intend to make. This is because increases in the capital stock have to be financed and there is an opportunity cost to that finance. Firms often borrow from banks to finance investment, so if interest rates rise the cost of borrowing rises and firms are less likely to borrow, and therefore less likely to invest. However, investment is not based solely on interest rates and some argue that the interest elasticity of demand for investment is very low. The prospects for future interest rates may be more significant than the current rate of interest and many firms watch closely the decisions on interest rates made by the Monetary Policy Committee (see p. 48).

Other main factors are demand for exports (a low exchange rate or a surging demand in a country to which a firm is trying to export) or access to credit (how keen banks are to lend, what conditions they apply to loans and how much of the risk is channelled into the rate of interest). However, much can be explained by a kind of irrational behaviour of humans keen to make profit or avoid losses, described by Keynes as animal spirits.

Keynes was an influential commentator on economic issues throughout and between the world wars, and in particular through the Wall Street Crash of 1929 and the Great Depression that followed. His ideas provide an opposing view to the Classical School, where human behaviour is deemed to be rational, markets are best left to themselves (laissez faire) and governments should have no discretionary or determining role in the level of *AD*. Keynes believed that it was not rational thinking that made people invest or sell in capital and stock markets. Instead, there is an animal or herd instinct. When people smell success, for example when stock markets or house prices rise, they buy. A rational person would sell when prices are high and make a profit. However, Keynes stated that our irrational instincts mean we buy when we see prices are rising. We sell when prices fall because, in a state of panic, we want to avoid further losses. This behaviour explains the enormous volatility in asset prices and means that speculative buying tends to exaggerate trends in the business cycle. This causes bubbles (which, by their nature, burst) and means that governments would do well to intervene to try to stop the extremities that occur when markets are left to their own devices.

A change in investment changes the level of *AD*, but a change in *AD* also changes the level of investment. This circular relationship can be analysed using the *accelerator* and, although this is not required knowledge for the exam, it is a useful way of evaluating the role of investment.

Animal spirits The forces that make markets move in large booms and busts, as people buy and sell impulsively rather than calmly, using purely rational behaviour.

Exam tip

Remember that investment is a determinant of *AD*. It is also, in part, determined by it.

Government expenditure (*G*)

Government expenditure in the UK comprises over 40% of all spending in the economy, totalling about £590 billion. However, as a component of *AD* it accounts for only around 25% because a large part of government expenditure is paid out as transfer payments, which are really a movement of spending power from taxpayers to other consumers (so features as consumption).

The main influence on government spending is the **trade cycle**. In a boom or period of high economic growth, government expenditure is likely to fall as there is less demand for Jobseeker's Allowance and other benefits to low income groups. Revenue from taxation is likely to rise too, so the government is expected to be able to run a budget (or fiscal) surplus during a boom.

Government spending does not need to equal tax revenue and the difference between them is known as a budget (or fiscal) deficit or surplus. The government can deliberately manipulate *AD* by overspending (running a budget deficit) when there is a slowdown in the economy, and vice versa in a boom. This discretionary **fiscal policy** is seen by many Keynesians as a way to prevent *AD* from collapsing in a recession, and fiscal policy can also be used to prevent bubbles in growth and markets from getting too big. Taxing more heavily in times of abundance is a useful way to put the brakes on the economy, although sometimes governments miscalculate the start of the boom and raise taxes too early. Similarly, net spending can be increased in a recession, which reverses the effects of demand deficiency.

Another factor to consider is the national debt, which is the accumulation of budget deficits over the years. Governments hope that the budget will balance over the course of the economic cycle for current spending at least (not investment), otherwise the government will accrue national debt. Interest payments have to be made on this and if the government continues to overspend there will be a cost for future generations. In the short run, however, there is some flexibility with the balance of the government's accounts.

> ### Exam tip
> If the government operates a loose or expansionary fiscal policy, government spending is greater than taxation. This might mean a rise in government spending or a fall in taxation, or that government spending is rising more quickly than taxation receipts.

The Keynesian view is that fiscal policy is a powerful tool in shifting *AD*, made much more effective by the working of the multiplier. In contrast, the Classical economists' view is that overspending by the government has a similar effect to printing more money — it is purely inflationary.

There is now some consensus that deliberate fiscal manipulation has a short-run impact, but only if wage demands and other cost pressures are kept in check. Until the credit crunch and recession hit the economy in general in 2008, there was much consensus that it is only really through supply-side policies that long-term improvements in equilibrium employment will be achieved, as the *AS* curve shifts to the right. With the prospect of a repeat of the economic depression that followed the

Trade cycle The pattern of economic growth which changes from booms to recessions or slow growth in a fairly regular pattern.

Fiscal policy The deliberate manipulation of government spending and taxation in order to influence the level of *AD* in the economy.

1929 crash, Keynesian expansionary budgets again became popular. As Keynes would say, 'in the long run we are all dead': that is, by the time the unemployed become employable, they will be past employment age, and sometimes the government must not sit by and let the economy go into a deep slump, but instead stimulate the circular flow through fiscal policy.

Net trade (X – M)

Main influences on the (net) trade balance

Exports represent an injection into the circular flow of income, in that the money paid for goods and services sold abroad enters the domestic flow of income. *Imports* mean that there is an outflow of money. Exports minus imports gives the total movement of funds, known as *net exports*. (If the value of imports is greater than the value of exports, this will be a negative figure, as in the UK.) There are several reasons why the value of net exports might change:

- The main driver for net exports is the level of *real income*.
- Consider a change in the *exchange rate*. If this increases in value against other currencies, imports become cheaper and exports more expensive on world markets. Over time, people respond to these relative price movements and the demand for exports falls and the demand for imports rises. A stronger currency worsens net exports, whereas a weaker currency improves the figure. However, in the short run the price elasticity of demand for exports and imports tends to be low. This may be because contracts have been signed for specific deals in international trade or because the traded components are a small percentage of firms' overall costs. For example, an Italian importer of BMW Minis will agree a price in advance of delivery from the UK. If the pound gets stronger against the euro, the price of the cars remains as per contract. Likewise, price elasticity of demand for imports may also be low because of a lack of available substitutes, as in the case of oil. Owing to the low price elasticity of demand for exports and imports, the initial impact of a change in the exchange rate may be the opposite of the one described above.
- A third major cause of changes in the value of net exports is changes in the *global economy*. For example, if there is a recession in the USA but the UK does not suffer a slowdown, the USA will buy fewer exports from the UK and will attempt to export more. Similarly, if there is inflation in the UK but not in other countries, net exports from the UK will worsen as UK goods become increasingly uncompetitive. A collapse in a stock market in another part of the world may also have direct effects on UK exports via wealth effects (see p. 34).
- The *degree of protectionism* is a fourth factor that determines net exports. This is discussed fully in Theme 4.
- Finally, *non-price factors*, such as quality and after-sales service, are major determinants of net exports. Germany, for example, cannot compete effectively on price, but the value of its exports exceeds that of any other country owing to its high quality of design and manufacture.

In summary, when any of the components of *AD* rises, the curve shifts to the right (Figure 3). The same happens if imports fall. In the UK these components do not usually fall, but they may rise more slowly during an economic slowdown, which means that the *AD* curve will still shift to the right but by increasingly smaller amounts.

> **Exam tip**
>
> When referring to *AD*, bear in mind the components *C* + *I* + *G* + (*X* – *M*) and try to find ways to refer to the multiplier.

As a useful evaluation point, it is wise to consider that the above analysis involves changes in *levels* rather than rates. For example, the first point refers to *levels* of real income. While levels might not fall, a slower increase (as China is now experiencing) means that UK exports will rise more slowly.

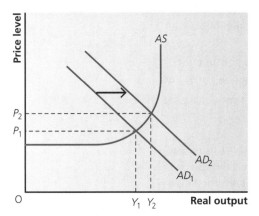

Figure 3 The effect of a shift in *AD* on price and real output

Aggregate supply (*AS*)

The characteristics of *AS*

Aggregate supply (*AS*) is the amount that firms are willing to produce at various price levels. It is largely influenced by productivity, which in turn is influenced by factors such as the costs of production, the level of investment, the availability and efficiency of factors of production and supply-side policies.

The distinction between movement along and a shift of the **AS** curve

There is a movement along the *AS* curve when the average price level changes. For example, if *AD* shifts to the right and the *AS* curve is relatively elastic, firms will be willing to produce more at slightly higher prices. However, if there is a change in the costs of production faced by all firms, the whole *AS* curve will shift. This might be because there is a change in the cost of raw materials, wages, exchange rates, indirect tax rates (short run) or changes in productive potential, for example because there are new fertilisers to make land more productive, a labour market is better educated, there is improved technology or there is investment in efficient capital assets (long run).

The relationship between short-run **AS** and long-run **AS**

Shifts in the short-run *AS* curve occur because there is a change in costs of production, but the overall productive capacity remains unchanged. The short run means that there is at least one fixed factor and firms cannot change their overall output unless the factors of production are variable. So short-run changes in *AS* might feed through to long-term changes. Long-run *AS* shows the productive potential of firms when all factors are variable. For a Classical economist, the long-run *AS* is a vertical line on the *AD/AS* diagram and it is the productive potential in an economy when all resources are used efficiently. For a Keynesian economist, the long-run *AS* incorporates the idea that there can be spare capacity or an output gap even in the long run because markets do not clear. In the long run, the ability of an economy

Exam tip

For the exam, you can draw the *AS* curve with straight lines and still earn all the available analysis marks. However, if you draw an *AS* curve with a sense of spare capacity, bottlenecks and full capacity (that is, an upward-sloping curve), you will find it easier to pick up evaluation marks.

to produce goods and services to meet demand is based on the state of production technology, the country's infrastructure and the quantity and quality of factors of production such as labour.

- Short-run 'supply-side shocks' cause a shift in the *short-run AS* curve. For example, changes in oil price or exchange rates.
- Changes in the quantity or quality of factors of production feed through into a shift in the long-run *AS* curve.
- Some factors such as a fall in oil prices can have a short-run and a long-run effect. The key difference is that the short-run impact is a change in production costs, but the long-run change is a new level of potential output.

Short-run *AS*

Shifts in *AS* occur when factors change that affect most firms. In the short run these changes simply affect firms' costs of production and not the amount that they are willing and able to produce. Short-run shifts are often called *external shocks* and cause *AS* to shift up or down rather than right or left (which indicates a change in capacity). These factors might relate specifically to the cost of workers (labour market) or the way in which firms compete (product market).

Short-run shifts might include:

- *Changes in costs of raw materials and energy.* In a developed country like the UK, most raw materials are imported and, if global competition increases, UK costs fall. The cost of these imports depends on demand pressures from other parts of the world as well as supply. If there is a global increase in demand for oil, for example, this causes the costs of production to increase in the UK because oil is a major production cost in almost all UK firms.
- *Changes in exchange rates.* If the euro falls in value relative to the pound, many costs would fall in the UK, meaning that *AS* in the UK increases.
- *Changes in tax rates.* If there is an increase in indirect taxes, there will be an increase in costs for almost all firms in the UK. A rise in VAT, for example, would be likely to make all prices go up as firms try to pass on these extra costs to the consumer. An increase in taxes is said to decrease the *AS* curve, i.e. push it upwards/leftwards. By contrast, a cut in the tax on petrol prices causes an increase in *AS*.

Long-run *AS*

Different shapes of the long-run AS curve

There are two views of *AS*. The Classical view is that in the long run an economy will operate at full capacity and there will be no unemployed resources in the economy, i.e. the *AS* curve is vertical. If there are any unemployed resources, the prices of these factors will fall until the surplus disappears, as long as there is no government intervention such as minimum wages.

By contrast, the Keynesian view is that the equilibrium level of output can occur below the full employment level of output. According to this view, the *AS* curve has a backward-bending L shape, with three distinct sections: spare capacity, **bottlenecks** and full capacity. The assumption behind this analysis is that an economy can be at

Bottlenecks Where restrictions in the capacity to increase production occur, meaning that prices will start to rise as output rises.

equilibrium when it is not at full employment. In other words, demand deficiency may mean that unemployed resources such as labour will not find work if the economy is left to its own devices.

In section A of Figure 4 there is spare capacity. The economy can increase output without any cost pressures. This is because there are unused resources such as factories not working at full capacity or unemployed labour. In this section, *AD* might shift to the right — for example, through fiscal policy — and equilibrium real output would increase without causing an increase in the price level. The situation is comparable to that of Japan over the past two decades, where there is a lot of scope for increased production but unemployment persists in the long run.

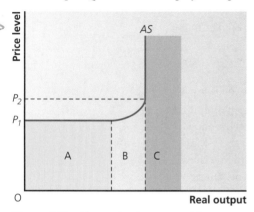

Figure 4 The Keynesian long-run *AS* curve

Section B is the bottlenecks section, where some constrictions in the supply chain cause cost and wage pressures to build up in some areas of the economy. This usually involves a certain type of labour which, when in short supply, can have its price bid upwards. An example concerns the shortage of construction workers associated with the High Speed 2 (HS2) rail link. If *AD* expands in this section of the graph, then although the economy will still grow, there will be some inflation because in order to attract enough construction workers the scheme operators will have to raise wages to draw workers away from other jobs, which will have effects on the production costs of *all* firms.

Section C illustrates full capacity in the economy. All viable workers have work, so if a firm wants to take on more workers it will have to entice them away from other jobs by offering higher wages. In this section of the diagram, if *AD* increases, although in the short run there might be some extra spending, the long-term effect will be increased inflation and no increased output.

According to the Classical view, section C is the only part of the *AS* curve that occurs. The economy cannot be in equilibrium while there is unemployment. So, if unemployment does exist, it can only result from a short-run failure of the market or from mismanagement by the government.

Knowledge check 23

Do all economists draw the *AS* curve as upward-sloping?

Many students get very confused when drawing *AD/AS* diagrams, either using microeconomic labels (*D* and *S*) or shifting *AD* and *AS* in the wrong directions. It is best to use simple versions of the diagrams that you understand.

Many *AD/AS* diagrams are drawn in exams — and, indeed, in some textbooks — with inflation rather than the price level on the vertical axis. Use the price level label for simplicity.

Factors influencing long-run AS

Let's consider how changes in both the labour market and the product market might produce a rightward shift of the *AS* curve (long-run shifts).

Labour market

In the labour market, a rightward shift in the *AS* curve could occur in the following ways:

- *Changes in relative productivity.* Productivity is output per unit of input and, if it increases relative to a country's main trading partners, the productivity gap is said to be closing. For example, the gap is currently closing between the UK and France, so although the UK has lower productivity than France, its productivity is increasing over time. This means that the costs of production are becoming relatively less expensive in the UK compared to France. However, the gap is widening between the UK and the rest of its major trading partners.
- *Changes in education and skills.* Increased spending on education and training should mean that a country's workforce can produce more output per worker. Education increases the value of the potential output. However, not all education achieves this end. It is not clear that a BA in Madonna Studies or a BSc in Surf Science has a major impact on costs of production in the UK.
- *Demographic changes and migration.* A decreasing birth rate and increasing life expectancy in the UK will have long-lasting impact on the labour force and changes in the supply of labour shift the *AS* curve as the costs and quality of labour change. The UK population has been rising — it is now at 64 million — and this is largely explained through net migration, i.e. more people have come to live in the UK than have left it. The effect of migration on employment and unemployment has been discussed on pp. 18–19, and the extent to which migrants impact on the labour force determines whether firms' costs will change as a whole.
- *Increases in health spending.* An increase in resources in the health sector should mean that workers have fewer days off sick and are active for longer — often beyond traditional retirement ages. However, spending on health might be absorbed into wage increases for staff in the health service, which would have little overall effect on the level of healthcare. Similarly, the majority of healthcare spending goes on the elderly or very young, neither of which are economically active.

Make sure that you know three supply-side policies in detail. Make sure they are not demand-side policies or trade policies. Remember that subsidies and privatisation might not be the best solutions to problems such as low levels of productivity in the current context for the UK.

Product market

In the product market, a rightward shift in the AS curve could occur in the following ways:

- *Technological advances*. Innovation and investment in new ideas tend to reduce costs for all firms. For example, widespread access to the internet increases competition among firms and means that firms can be more streamlined. Buying a book, for example, is now much cheaper online because there are fewer expensive retail outlets to maintain.

- *Changes in government regulation*. There are many regulations in the UK economy that have been imposed to try to maintain a disciplined economy such as in the postal and telecommunications services. However, such industries have been increasingly deregulated over the past two decades to increase competition, which in turn imposes its own form of discipline. The net effect is that parcel postage and phone services — costs faced by all firms — have reduced in real terms, shifting AS to the right.

- *Competition policy and reduction in barriers to international trade*. As a country opens up to more trade, competition drives down prices and inefficient domestic firms give way to overseas firms with a comparative advantage. Therefore, as globalisation develops, AS increases.

Exam tip

You will be required to draw *AD/AS* diagrams in your exam, so you might like to sketch all the possible permutations and put them on separate cards. Then rank them in order of the way in which you would use them to solve various macroeconomic problems.

Knowledge checks 24–26

For each of the following, decide whether *AD* or *AS* changes, or both. Then decide whether they increase or decrease. Are these short-term or long-term changes?

24 A cut in education spending.

25 A rise in interest rates.

26 An increase in productivity relative to the UK's main export markets.

Links and common themes

- The relationship between exchange rates and net exports can most clearly be understood using the Marshall–Lerner condition and the J curve. This will be explained in Theme 4.
- Fiscal policy is discussed further on pp. 47–50 of this guide, and developed more fully in Theme 4.

Summary

- *AD* is the total amount that is planned to be spent in an economy at any price level.
- *AS* is the output that all firms are willing to supply at any price level.
- Equilibrium real output and price level occur where *AD* meets *AS*.
- The components of *AD* are $C + I + G + (X - M)$ and a change in any one of these will shift the *AD* curve, with multiplier effects.

- If *AD* increases, the price level is likely to rise and output may rise, depending on the price elasticity of the *AS* curve.
- Increases in *AS* tend to lower prices or curb rises in prices. Real output is likely to increase, although this depends on the elasticities where the *AD* and *AS* curves cross.

National income

The circular flow of income

Imagine the economy as a simple model where there are just households and firms. The households own all the factors of production — land, labour, capital and enterprise — and the firms are the producing units. Money moves from households to firms when they buy goods and services; and money moves back to households as payment for the use of the factors of production in the form of rent, wages, interest and profit. In this very simple model, known as the *circular flow of income* (Figure 5), money circulates from households to firms and back again, and the more that households spend and the more that firms produce, the higher the levels of income. It does not matter which way you look at it, the income and output in an economy should always be the same, and they are measured by gross domestic product (GDP).

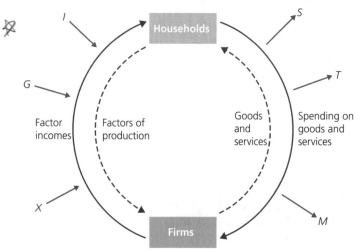

Figure 5 The circular flow of income

The distinction between income and wealth

Wealth is the sum of all the assets in an economy. In the UK, most wealth is held in the form of housing (almost 60%); the other major forms of wealth are stocks and shares and capital assets. Wealth is a stock concept, whereas *income* is a flow concept — this means that wealth does not have a direct impact on the circular flow of income, but changes in wealth have an effect on incomes and spending (the **wealth effect**). For example, if you live in a property that increases in value, you might feel more confident about spending in the economy and your increased spending will then become part of the circular flow of income. Moreover, if houses become more expensive, someone could go to their mortgage provider and request mortgage equity release, i.e. take out a loan based on the increased wealth. When that loan is spent, the circular flow increases. By contrast, when capital markets take a downturn in the USA, for example, people living on pensions in the UK might find that their incomes fall because dividends on pension funds are often based on capital gains of shares.

Wealth effect The effect on incomes or spending when asset values change.

Knowledge check 27

Is it true that an increase in house prices (wealth) causes a fall in *AD* because people don't have as much money to spend on other things?

Injections and withdrawals

There are three **injections** into the circular flow of income: investment (I) (an increase in the capital stock), government spending (G) and exports (X). These all increase the circular flow and a change in any will be magnified by the multiplier (see below).

There are three **withdrawals** (leakages) from the circular flow of income: savings (S), tax (T) and imports (M). If you hide your money under your bed, the economy slows down a little because there is less money in the circular flow. Similarly, if the government takes money away from the economy in the form of tax and does not spend it, or if people buy more things from abroad than they export, the economy slows down as money leaves the circular flow. These three leakages effectively determine the size of the multiplier.

If all the injections equal all the leakages, then the economy will be in equilibrium; if injections are greater than leakages, the economy will grow; and if leakages are greater than injections, the economy will contract.

Equilibrium levels of real national output

When AD meets AS there is an *equilibrium* point, which tells us the price level and real GDP of a country. An equilibrium is a balancing point where there is no tendency to change the price level or output level. When there is a shift in AD or AS, there is a movement away from the original equilibrium to form a new equilibrium, as follows:

- If prices were higher than the new equilibrium (or point at which the new AD and AS cross), there would be a tendency for prices to fall because supply would be greater than demand and there would be lots of unsold goods and services.
- If prices were lower than the new equilibrium, there would be shortages and prices would start to rise in order to make sure that everyone could get what they were prepared to pay for.
- If, for example, a worldwide recession and a fall in AD occurred, you would expect to see falls in prices (or that prices did not rise very quickly).

> **Exam tip**
>
> Sketch an *AD/AS* diagram and mark on the equilibrium point. Shift *AD* or *AS*, and then mark on the new equilibrium. Use the concept of surpluses and deficits to show the movement from one equilibrium to the other, as explained here.

The multiplier

The *multiplier ratio* is the ratio of a change in equilibrium real income to the autonomous change (the injection) that brought it about. In other words, it is the number of times a change in incomes exceeds the change in net injections that caused it. It is the knock-on effect on incomes when injections and withdrawals change. For example, if there is a £10 million increase in export values, the inward flow of money to the UK will be re-spent within the UK. When the money is spent, it becomes other people's incomes. These incomes will be re-spent, and so on.

Injections Flows into the circular flow of income comprising investment, government spending and exports.

Withdrawals Flows out of the circular flow of income comprising savings, tax and imports.

Knowledge check 28

Is consumption an injection into the circular flow?

The most important factor in determining the size of the multiplier is the size of the withdrawals from the circular flow, i.e. what proportion of the additional income is saved by households, what proportion is spent on imported goods and what proportion is paid to the government in the form of taxation.

The multiplier is inversely proportional to the **marginal propensity to withdraw (MPW)**, i.e. it is:

$$\frac{1}{MPW}$$

MPW is the proportion of one unit of additional national income which is withdrawn from the circular flow, or the sum of the *marginal propensity to save (MPS)*, *marginal propensity to tax (MPT)* and *marginal propensity to import (MPM)*, which can be summarised as MPS + MPT + MPM. Therefore, the formula for the multiplier can also be written as:

$$\text{Multiplier} = \frac{1}{MPS + MPT + MPM}$$

Perhaps the most efficient way to write this is as:

$$\text{Multiplier} = \frac{1}{(1 - MPC)}$$

where MPC stands for the **marginal propensity to consume**.

If you add together the MPC and MPW you get 1, i.e. the total amount. Therefore if MPC + MPW = 1, a rearrangement of the formula gives the value of MPW as (1 − MPC).

The importance of the multiplier is that if there is any change in spending in an economy, the final impact on incomes will be much greater than the initial impact. The greater the leakages, the smaller the multiplier. The formula is based on how much of any extra pound earned is re-spent within the economy, i.e. the marginal propensity to consume (MPC). The size of the multiplier in the UK is approximately 1.4, but in developing countries it is often higher, which partly explains their higher growth rates. For example, in a country with a multiplier of 3, a net injection of $10 million causes a $30 million increase in incomes in total.

The larger the value of the multiplier, the greater the shift in *AD*. For example, if the multiplier is 1.1, a 100 trillion yen injection into the economy by the Japanese prime minister Shinzo Abe will have a 110 trillion yen positive impact on *AD*. However, if the multiplier is 2.0 the effect is 200 trillion yen. This can be both in a positive and a negative direction. So an increase in leakages, for example because imports rise, will have a larger negative impact on *AD*, according to the size of the multiplier.

Marginal propensity to withdraw (MPW) A measure of how much of any extra pound earned is saved, taxed or spent outside the economy on imports.

Marginal propensity to consume (MPC) A measure of how much of any extra pound earned is spent within the economy.

Useful exercises

- Do some calculations with the multiplier ratio. This is a new part of the specification and it is therefore likely to be examined early on in the new series. The calculations are easy once you have done a few.
- A good site for mortgage information is the BBC website (www.bbc.co.uk). On the News page go to 'Business', then 'Economy', or watch a recent clip under 'Watch/Listen'.
- You might also visit the website of the Council of Mortgage Lenders at www.cml.org.uk or Mortgage Guide UK at www.mortgageguideuk.co.uk for accessible explanations and arguments about anything to do with mortgages.

Summary

- Income (e.g. export income) is a flow concept, whereas wealth (e.g. capital assets) is a stock concept. Income is measured in real GDP. Wealth in the UK is £6.7 trillion: five times the total income in the economy. See the gov.uk website at www.statistics.gov.uk for the latest figures.
- Most income in the UK is held in the form of housing (60%). The rest is split fairly equally between capital assets and shares. Capital assets or stock in the UK amount to £3.1 trillion. This is slightly less than the cost of maintaining all capital stocks in their current condition — a cost known as depreciation.

- Changes in income have multiplier effects on the level of total spending in the economy. An increase in injections has a proportionately larger effect on GDP.
- Changes in leakages affect the size of the multiplier. The larger the leakages, the smaller the multiplier effect will be.

Economic growth

Causes of growth

The distinction between actual and potential growth

Actual economic growth is an increase in real GDP and potential economic growth is an increase in capacity in the economy. Measures of real GDP tend to fluctuate over the course of an economic cycle. During a *boom*, real GDP rises fast. During a *recession*, it falls for at least two consecutive quarters. During a *slowdown*, the level of GDP may be rising, but rising below the trend, or GDP might be falling.

Factors which could cause economic growth

Actual economic growth can occur because there is an increase in one of the components of aggregate demand — consumption (*C*), investment (*I*), government expenditure (*G*) and net trade (*X* – *M*):

$$AD = C + I + G + (X - M)$$

Here are some examples. Increased consumption might occur because of increased consumer confidence or the availability of credit. Increased investment increases the level of growth and is itself dependent on the level of growth (i.e. it has an accelerating effect on growth rates). Government spending on education or health might cause growth. Export-led growth has the added advantage of improving the current account of the balance of payments.

Actual economic growth can also occur because of an increase in aggregate supply (*AS*). This might happen because costs of production fall (e.g. labour markets might become more competitive thanks to immigration or an increase in the birth rate) or because of government supply-side policy such as *deregulation* in the markets (removing constraints that limit competition).

A shift in the *AD* or *AS* curve to the right should cause an increase in actual growth. However, if *AD* increases and the *AD* curve is crossing the vertical part of the *AS* curve, the only effect will be increased prices not increased GDP. Similarly, if *AS* increases and the *AD* curve is crossing the *AS* curve on its horizontal part, there will be no change in the equilibrium and there will be no change in price levels or output.

Potential economic growth

Potential economic growth can only occur when the vertical part of the *AS* curve shifts to the right, increasing the amount that the economy could produce. Using another model, potential economic growth increases when the production possibility curve shifts outwards. Possible causes of the *AS* shift are described in a previous section on pp. 32–33.

> **Exam tip**
>
> Economic growth is most useful to economists when presented without the effects of inflation, i.e. as real or constant values. If you are given nominal or current values, you will gain marks by commenting that the figures are distorted by inflation.

Actual economic growth An increase in real GDP.

Potential economic growth An increase in capacity in the economy.

Export-led growth The economic growth caused by rises in net exports. It has the benign effect of stimulating the domestic economy while improving the trade balance.

The importance of international trade for (export-led) economic growth

Knowledge check 29

What is the difference between actual and potential economic growth?

Export-led growth — where the driver of growth is an increase in the export component of *AD* — is a main driver of growth in many economies. For countries that have been rapidly emerging into industrialised states such as China, exports can often account for more than 50% of *AD*. Export-led growth means that the balance of payments will improve as more goods and services are sold abroad.

The main problem with export-led growth is that it makes the exporters vulnerable to changes in demand in other countries, or exchange rates, both of which are often outside their control. China's growth slowed significantly as a result of the global financial crisis in 2008 and in order to maintain its exports the government decided to intervene to keep the currency, the renminbi, from rising against other countries. Currency market interventions are not popular in terms of the world trade climate.

Constraints on growth

There are several factors constraining growth:

■ *Absence of efficient capital markets*. One of the main reasons why Latin America grows more slowly than the Asian subcontinent is that Asia has more credible and efficient capital markets. In many economies in sub-Saharan Africa, the interest charged on credit, if credit is available at all, is typically over 50%. One of the issues is the *asymmetric information* in credit markets, where the lender knows very little about the borrower and charges higher rates to cover the enormous risk. The only people able to afford these high rates are likely to be among the more corrupt borrowers, which makes it even less likely that people will lend. The market then becomes a *missing market*, in the sense that there is no equilibrium price of credit where buyers and sellers can agree a rate of interest.

■ *Government instability*. Where governments are incompetent, or lack transparency or strong political backing, the economy cannot attract inward investment and the currency might be unstable. The government might have a fiscal deficit, which means that it has little power to spend money to encourage growth. This is more extreme if there is political tension, wars or diversion of funds to increase a country's defence.

■ *Labour market problems*. A shortage of skilled labour is a major constraint on growth. As countries get richer, birth rates tend to fall dramatically; in the long run this means that the labour supply will fall. One of the most effective policies for reducing this in high-income countries is to allow increased immigration, although in low-income countries the exit of skilled workers (known as the 'brain drain') exacerbates the skill problems.

■ *External constraints*. Trade is a key driver of growth. Uneven access to world markets owing to tariffs and subsidies can prevent a country from growing. Global recession or fears of terrorism also slow down trade, as does volatility in exchange rate markets. Figures suggest that for every 3% growth in world trade there is a 1% increase in world GDP, and therefore anything that holds back international trade is likely to act as a constraint on growth.

Output gaps

Distinction between actual growth rates and long-term trends

The difference between actual output and either the trend or potential output is called the output gap. If there is an output gap, the country is not growing at the trend of the potential output. One way of drawing the output gap is shown in Figure 6.

Output gap The difference between actual and potential GDP or growth in GDP.

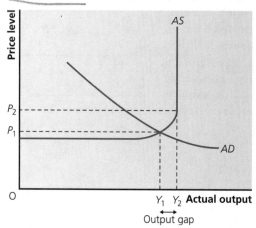

Figure 6 The output gap shown as the difference between actual output and potential output

Positive and negative output gaps and difficulties of measurement

If the economy is growing faster than the trend, pressures will grow in the economy, such as tight labour markets, wage pressures and shortages of raw materials. This is referred to as a *positive output gap*. It may be a sign that the economy is overheating and the inflationary pressures might persuade the Bank of England's Monetary Policy Committee to raise interest rates. However, if the economy is growing below trend, there is likely to be spare capacity in the economy. This situation is known as a *negative output gap*. It means that there is scope for a cut in interest rates, which is less likely to cause inflationary pressures.

You can find estimates of the output gap by looking at the Bank of England's Inflation Report or the data from the IMF, the OECD or the Office for Budget Responsibility. The Bank of England's report in May 2014 estimated the gap to be around 1.5%, based on the unemployment figures (7%). Other sources such as Oxford Economics (an independent forecaster) put the figure as 4–5%. As you will gather from this, it is difficult to estimate the size of the output gap because not all unemployed resources would have the same impact on the economy if they were eventually employed. To make the situation more complicated, the non-use of resources makes them less useable in the future and the productive potential of the economy tends to fall when there are high levels of unemployment. This is shown by a shift down in the path of potential or trend growth, which might be illustrated as shown in Figure 7.

Exam tip

A negative output gap means that the country is not using its resources to the full. There could be an increase in output without opportunity cost in terms of inflation.

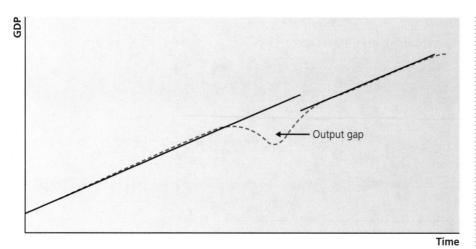

Figure 7 The 'shifting size' of the output gap as potential growth declines

Use of *AD/AS* diagram to illustrate an output gap

The output gap is a measure of the difference between actual and potential growth in the economy. It is based on estimates of what the production possibility of the country is relative to the actual GDP. One way in which Keynesian economists illustrate the output gap is as follows. To illustrate the country's production possibility, draw a level of output through the vertical part of the long-run *AS* curve (Y_{FE}). For Keynesians, the *AS* curve is a curve that is not vertical but upward-sloping, as shown in Figure 8. To then plot the output gap, we can show the difference between actual output (where *AD* equals *AS* at Y_1) and the full capacity potential.

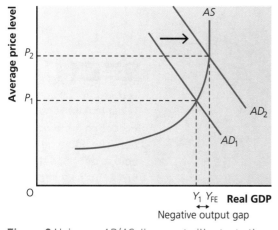

Figure 8 Using an *AD/AS* diagram to illustrate the output gap

Keynesians believe that a negative output gap can exist in the long run as well as the short run, but Classical economists believe that output gaps do not exist in the long run because the long-run *AS* is vertical through Y_{FE} (full employment output). The actual size of the output gap is measured by the Office for Budget Responsibility, as shown in Figure 9.

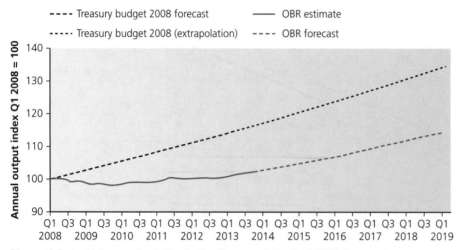

Figure 9 Potential output relative to the Treasury's budget 2008 forecast

Source: ONS and Office for Budget Responsibility

Trade (business) cycle

The *trade cycle*, also called the economic or business cycle, demonstrates recurring trends in economic growth rates, as shown in Figure 10. *Booms* tend to be followed by economic slumps or slowdowns, which tend to be followed by *recession*, before the economy moves into the recovery phase, and then back into a boom.

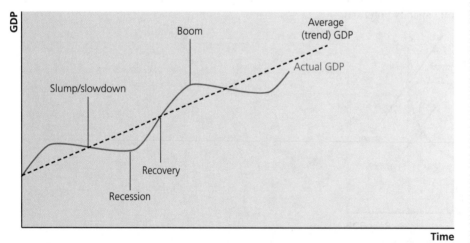

Figure 10 A stylised diagram of the trade cycle

This trend is explained in part by animal spirits — Keynes's term for the speculative action that results from any rise or fall in output or asset prices (see p. 26). However, other reasons can explain the trend such as the effects of changes in capital which exacerbate changes in output and the role of expectations in the decision-making of businesses.

Exam tip

You will not be required to explain why the economic cycle occurs, but you should be able to describe the problems that result from it (such as unemployment, fiscal imbalances or bubbles in asset prices such as houses) and the ways in which governments might address these problems.

The impact of economic growth

Benefits

Growth benefits consumers, firms, governments and living standards in the following ways:

- *Consumers.* Incomes and wealth rise when there is economic growth. It also means that people can afford to save money for their future consumption. People feel more confident about their jobs when growth is high, so they are more willing to spend on consumer durables such as cars or gadgets. There are likely to be more employment opportunities so that people can progress in their careers, either within their own company or in another. Wages might rise as firms try to keep hold of their workers.
- *Firms.* Firms tend to make more profit when there is economic growth. In times of growth, consumer spending usually rises, which means that firms sell more. As revenues and profits rise, firms can take on more workers and are more likely to invest. This increases future growth prospects.
- *Governments.* When incomes and assets rise in price, people pay more income tax, VAT and capital gains tax. Firms will pay more corporation tax. Governments also have fewer demands to pay unemployment benefits and income support. So in times of economic growth the government is likely to enjoy a healthier fiscal position.
- *Current and future living standards.* Growth means that total incomes are rising in an economy, so this is likely to make people feel better off. Poverty rates are likely to fall as wages and employment rise. The government may decide to spend more of its income on areas that will increase living standards for all such as opening libraries or making town centres more pleasant. Firms might use cleaner technology because they can afford to, possibly motivated by improving their image for corporate social responsibility, thereby possibly increasing benefits to themselves and living standards more widely. Standards of living rise as long as the costs of living do not increase at the same rate. In other words, real growth means that real incomes rise. Increases in growth can mean that wealth in the form of assets such as shares and houses increases.

Costs

Despite the benefits listed above, growth can incur the following costs:

- *Income inequality.* The unwaged and unskilled are less likely to benefit from increased incomes. Although money might eventually trickle down to lower income groups, there might equally be a two-speed economy where the incomes of some people accelerate but others cannot get out of a low-skill slow lane. The type of production tends to change during periods of economic growth, so there is likely to be short-term unemployment for people who do not have labour market flexibility.
- *Environmental problems.* Depletion of natural resources and external costs such as carbon emissions and other forms of pollution are likely to increase with economic growth. However, high income governments can use their increased tax revenue to clean up the environment, and enforce carbon control measures.
- *Balance of payments problems on the current account.* With higher incomes, domestic consumers suck in more imports and there is less incentive for firms to export. However, if growth were export-led, the current account would improve.

> **Exam tip**
>
> Ensure you know some arguments for and against economic growth and can make a decision as to whether the benefits outweigh the costs.

- *Bottlenecks in the economy*. When there is little spare capacity in the economy, factors of production such as skilled labour and fuel rise in price. Monopoly power might also develop, which can be used as a barrier to the entry of new firms (for more on this, see Theme 3). This can be shown using an increasingly inelastic AS curve.
- *Social dislocation and stress*. Higher incomes will be earned by some, but not all. With increased pay there are usually increased responsibilities and expectations that money will be spent such as on mobile phone contracts for children, which can cause problems for low-income families – for example, increased household debt. There may be more travel and the need to move further afield as firms grow. However, with higher incomes people can afford to work fewer hours, go on more luxurious holidays, pay for their children's education or retire early. So social life may or may not improve as the economy grows.
- *Problems of rapid growth*. Rapid growth can cause short-term spikes in prices. If a country grows too quickly, there might be bad planning, corner cutting and shoddy workmanship. However, rapid growth might just need time to settle down in terms of income distribution and a strong government such as that in China can ensure that growth is planned effectively.

Knowledge check 30

Is there any validity in saying 'If there is increased growth, there will be inflation'?

Useful exercises

- Figures for the output gap in OECD countries are published by the OECD every year. In these figures, a positive output gap is a boom and a negative output gap is a slump. Find one country that has a positive output gap and another that has a negative output gap at the current time.
- Read an account of London in the winter of 1947, where smog brought the capital to a standstill. To what extent can economic growth be used to explain problems of smog and the cleanliness of much of London in recent years?

Links and common themes

- Asymmetric information (in capital markets) has been introduced in Theme 1 and is useful for explaining limits to growth.
- Constraints on growth in developing countries will be discussed fully when considering limits to growth and development in Theme 4.

Summary

- Economic growth can be explained in terms of increases in actual GDP or increases in potential GDP. When *AD* increases, actual GDP increases, as long as the *AS* curve is not vertical. When *AS* increases, actual GDP increases, as long as the *AD* curve does not cross the *AS* curve on a horizontal part of the curve. Only a shift in the *AS* curve to the right causes an increase in potential economic growth.

- The benefits and costs of growth are not easy to measure and they change over time. It is therefore difficult, but important, to assess whether the benefits outweigh the costs. As growth rates rise, it is likely that the increasing marginal costs will be outweighed by decreasing marginal benefits.

■ Macroeconomic objectives and policies

Possible macroeconomic objectives

There are seven main objectives that governments generally wish to pursue:

- economic growth (rises in real GDP)
- reduction in unemployment
- control of inflation
- equilibrium in the balance of payments on the current account
- balanced government budget
- protection of the environment
- more equal distribution of income

The order of priority varies according to the politics of the government in office at the time and institutional arrangements such as the Monetary Policy Committee. Some governments see the control of inflation as the most important macroeconomic goal. Others, such as governments with a socialist leaning, focus on the redistribution of income and the reduction of unemployment.

Demand-side policies

Distinction between monetary and fiscal policies

A demand-side policy is a deliberate manipulation by the government of AD in order to achieve macroeconomic objectives. There are two demand-side policies:

- *monetary policy*, which is decision-making using monetary instruments such as the interest rate and quantitative easing
- *fiscal policy*, which is the government's management of its spending and taxation with the aim of changing the total level of spending in the economy

Monetary policy instruments

The manipulation of monetary variables such as the interest rate has enormous implications across the whole economy. In the UK a group of up to nine economists forming the Bank of England's Monetary Policy Committee (MPC), whose sole purpose is the control of inflation, makes the interest rate decision independently of the government. They meet at least once a month for a day and a half to examine evidence from across the country relating to inflationary pressures. They have a target for CPI inflation set for them by the Chancellor of the Exchequer, currently at 2%. If inflation falls outside the range of 1–3%, the Governor of the Bank of England must write an open letter to the Chancellor to explain why this has happened. In its first 10 years of operation, this occurred only once when inflation reached 3.1% in March 2007, but between 2008 and 2011 he had to write 10 such letters (he only has to write one every three months if inflation remains above the ceiling or below the floor). Since 2011 the Governor has had much less explaining to do as CPI inflation has been in the range of 1–3% and, while the recession in the eurozone persisted, under 2%.

> **Exam tip**
>
> The MPC has a single target: inflation. It is incorrect to say that it aims to reduce unemployment or indeed has any other macroeconomic policy objective, although if inflation is under control this might allow other areas of the economy to benefit from lower interest rates.

Content Guidance

There are two major tools available to the MPC. The first is changing the base rate of interest — the Bank Rate, which is a benchmark for other interest rates in the money market. The second, used only since 2009, is quantitative easing, which can be used alongside the manipulation of the interest rate.

Interest rates

The MPC sets the Bank Rate each month and the objective of monetary policy to meet the government's 2% inflation target. Changing the rate of interest sets off a chain of reactions in the economy, many of which mean that AD will shift. We call these processes monetary 'transmissions mechanisms'. This means that there are processes which, step by step, mean that an interest rate transmits to a change in demand. These mechanisms work through consumption, for example by affecting how much money people have after paying their mortgage. Also, consumers spend different amounts depending on the cost of credit and the amount that they receive for their savings. Investment is sensitive to interest rate changes: higher rates mean that fewer projects are deemed to be worthwhile. Net exports are also affected by interest rate changes, not just because interest rates affect costs of production and therefore relative productivity. The other factor is that interest rate changes are likely to affect exchange rates, which have an immediate impact on export and import prices.

Quantitative easing

The MPC announced in March 2009 that it would start to inject money directly into the economy to boost spending — a policy known as **quantitative easing (QE)**. It began purchasing financial assets (long-term loans called *gilts*), funded by the creation of central bank reserves which are paid for by selling Treasury bills (short-term 90-day loans), which are effectively cash as they are so easily turned into cash. It is what the media call 'printing money', but it is more honest and fair than that term implies. The Bank's asset purchases are designed to inject money directly into the economy to raise asset prices (which keeps yields, or interest on government bonds, low), boost spending and so keep inflation on track to meet the 2% target.

QE was needed because spending in the economy slowed very sharply in the latter part of 2008 and during 2009 as the global financial crisis gathered pace. This threatened a downward spiral through a combination of contracting real output and price deflation. The MPC responded decisively, cutting the Bank Rate from 5% to 0.5% — its lowest ever level — in just 5 months to reduce the risk of inflation falling below the 2% target. But more was needed, which is why QE came in.

How does QE work?

As a result of QE, asset holders in general — including households and businesses — will have portfolios with higher value and more liquidity (assets that are easy to transfer into cash). If they feel wealthier and have more money immediately available, they are more likely to increase their spending, boosting AD. In turn, consumers and businesses may be encouraged to take on more debt because lower yields on financial assets — in other words, lower interest rates — bring down the cost of borrowing.

However, there are factors that may work to dampen the effects of QE. One is the nature of the banking sector. The boost to the value of banks' asset holdings and their holdings of liquid assets as a result of QE, by itself, might be expected to make them more willing to lend. However, after the global financial crisis, banks are concerned

Exam tip

When you consider a rise in interest rates, remember that the value of the exchange rate is likely to change in the same direction. For example, if interest rates rise, the value of the pound is likely to rise.

Exam tip

With a **s**trong **p**ound **i**mports are **c**heap and **e**xports are **d**ear, which can be remembered by the acronym SPICED.

Quantitative easing (QE) The purchase of gilts and other illiquid assets as a means of making credit easier to access.

about their financial health and as a result are less willing to lend. For this reason, the MPC did not expect QE to result in a material expansion of bank lending.

A second round of asset purchases, known as QE2, was agreed by the MPC in October 2011 as output growth had weakened. This made it more likely than not that inflation would undershoot the 2% target without further monetary stimulus. The MPC voted unanimously to purchase a further round of gilt purchases, bringing the stock of purchases to £375 billion. By 2015 the inflation rate reached an important milestone of 0%.

Exiting QE as the economy recovers

As the economic recovery becomes stronger and more enduring, the appropriate settings of monetary policy needed to deliver the inflation target will change. This means that, at some point, the MPC will begin to tighten and the QE asset purchases will be resold in the money markets, or allowed to 'taper' as the assets start to mature and are not replaced. This will have the effect of tightening monetary policy, making easy credit less available. Over time, as the economy continues to recover, you will see the bonds being resold in the market — a process that will have a similar effect as raising the interest rate.

Monetary policy involves controlling inflation, whether too high or too low. To judge whether the policy is worth pursuing, it is helpful to consider the costs of inflation and the possible benefits of a little inflation. See 'The effects of inflation' on pp. 13–14.

> **Exam tip**
>
> For your exam you need to know that monetary policy involves the manipulation of interest rates to achieve economic objectives. However, monetary policy can also involve quantitative easing and you can gain valuable marks if you discuss the use of increasing liquidity as a way of easing credit.

Fiscal policy instruments

Fiscal policy is the manipulation of taxes and government spending to influence the overall level of demand in an economy. Expansionary policy means cutting tax (T) or raising government spending (G) or a combination of the two, so that the net effect of the government's budget is that AD rises. Contractionary policy means that T is greater than G.

Distinction between government budget deficit and surplus

If government spending is greater than taxation, the government is operating a **budget (or fiscal) deficit**. The net effect is to pump spending power into the economy. The *multiplier* magnifies the effect of this boost. For example, if the government builds a new hospital and does not pay for it all through current taxation but instead borrows to finance the scheme, there will effectively be more spending power in the economy at the expense of spending power in the future. When the government pays for the workers and building materials for this hospital, the incomes will be re-spent in the economy, creating new incomes — which is the multiplier in operation. If an economy is going through a slowdown or recession, according to Keynesian thinking the government should spend its way out of the recession.

By contrast, if government spending is less than taxation, there is said to be a **budget (or fiscal) surplus**, which takes spending power out of the economy with negative multiplier effects. The consensus among economists is that in times of boom or fast growth in the economy, the government should rein in its spending to curb inflationary pressures. This is known as *contractionary fiscal policy* and it puts the government's accounts in a better position.

> **Budget (or fiscal) deficit** The amount by which government spending exceeds revenues. The UK has run a budget deficit since 2001.

> **Budget (or fiscal) surplus** The amount by which tax revenues exceed government spending. The next budget surplus in the UK is expected in 2018.

Distinction between direct and indirect taxation

The governments can change fiscal policy by changing its tax or spending levels, or both. Within the tax changes it can change *direct tax*, which is tax on incomes (e.g. income tax, corporation tax) or *indirect tax*, which is tax on spending (e.g. VAT).

A direct tax will have an impact on AD because people feel better or worse off according to how much income changes. We make spending plans based on our *disposable income*, i.e. income after tax. Although the changes in direct tax might not have an immediate effect, there is the compounded effect of expectations and confidence. If direct taxes are raised, we would expect AD to be subdued.

An indirect tax has a more obvious effect on AS because it affects the amount that firms are willing to sell at any particular price. Many firms have to absorb some of the effects of a rise in VAT, for example, so will be less willing to sell when VAT is raised. We show this by a short-run upwards shift (decrease) in the AS curve.

> ### Links and common themes
>
> The decision as to which tax is changed is a major part of Theme 4. For Theme 2 you need to remember that direct taxes can shift AD and indirect taxes tend to shift AS.

The role and operation of the Bank of England's MPC

When interest rates are raised, the cost of borrowing rises. Consumers who borrow in order to finance their spending might be deterred from doing so and savers will be less keen to spend their savings because there is a greater opportunity cost in so doing. People with mortgages — of whom there are almost 10 million in the UK — will find their mortgage interest repayments rise and will therefore be discouraged from spending, although those with fixed-rate mortgages will not suffer this immediately. Hire purchase — the method of buying major durable items, such as cars and white goods, on credit — will incur increasingly expensive monthly repayment instalments, which means that consumers might delay further major expenditures. House prices may fall as mortgages become less affordable and this can cause negative wealth effects, where lower asset prices mean that people feel less inclined to spend and less able to take out loans based on the equity in their homes.

Firms will find that investment is less attractive in many cases and that fewer investments will make a return higher than the increased cost of borrowing. Therefore, firms will be less inclined to invest, which not only reduces current AD but also has implications for long-term output prospects. The cost of exports might increase because interest rates are essentially a cost of production, so exports will fall and imports will rise. This is made even more likely when we factor in a probable increase in the exchange rate, which occurs when 'hot money' is attracted to higher interest rates in the UK.

All these changes shift the AD curve to the left with multiplier effects. Depending on the shape of the AS curve, this may decrease both the price level and real output. Increasing interest rates can be an effective way of controlling inflation, but the cost is that economic growth is subdued.

Demand-side policies in the Great Depression and the 2008 global financial crisis

The Wall Street Crash of 1929 triggered a worldwide crash in stock markets and a global recession, much like the 2008 experience. Back in 1929 Keynes was very influential in terms of policy responses both in the USA and the UK. Expansionary fiscal policy was used to bring back some confidence in markets and stop the spiral downwards of demand and output. The UK did not respond as quickly as the USA, and it was not until the post-war period, under a Labour Government, that demand-side policies became significantly expansionary.

By 1968, however, Keynes's ideas had become discredited. The problem with expansion is that it had led to inflation. After expansionary policies had been used and the result was inflation, the brakes were put on and demand was crushed back. This so-called 'stop-go' policy meant that the UK experienced both inflation and unemployment at the same time. A new term emerged, stagflation, meaning stagnant inflation. Milton Friedman in Chicago wrote that expansionary fiscal policy would only cause inflation and the effects on the jobs market would only be short term, and the government should not use demand-side policies at all to influence the level of output and employment. Friedman's ideas were popular on both sides of the Atlantic up until 2008.

Stagflation A stagnant (not growing) economy that is also suffering from inflation.

The policy responses post the 2008 crisis were broadly similar in the USA and the UK until 2010. In the USA President Obama was clearly a Keynesian, using fiscal policy to expand the economy by getting involved in major infrastructure projects across the country. In the UK the Labour Government under Gordon Brown was similarly keen to increase spending and the deficit in 2008 rose from under 40% of GDP to well above 80%. However, everything changed in 2010 when the Labour Party lost the general election and the new Coalition Government made fiscal balance one of its main short-term objectives. Austerity in a recession followed. US growth soared, but there are different views on the UK experience. It did not experience the double-dip recession that was widely predicted and, although growth was initially slow, by 2014 growth was up to the levels seen in the USA.

> **Exam tip**
>
> You can hold your own view on whether demand-side policies are effective in the aftermath of a credit crash and to prevent a deep recession. Remember that, whatever your view, make sure you can see the other side of the argument.

Strengths and weaknesses of demand-side policies

How effective is monetary policy?

Monetary policy has a shorter time lag than fiscal policy, although the MPC estimates that interest rate changes can take 18 months to 2 years to have their full impact. There are further time delays because many mortgage holders have fixed-rate policies, which may delay the impact on their spending for some years. Furthermore, monetary policy is a blunt tool that hits the whole economy, affecting both small and large firms, and rises in interest rates usually worsen income distribution. However, perhaps the most significant criticism of monetary policy is that it raises the costs of production in a situation where the cause of inflation may itself be an increase in costs. So the rise in interest rates, rather than curing the problem, exacerbates it. At a time of rising commodity prices, those who have to bear the brunt of this are people in debt. The evidence suggests that the first round of QE in 2009 raised the level of real GDP by 1–2% and increased inflation by between 0.75% and 1%.

Does fiscal policy work?

In the UK fiscal policy can only be implemented in the annual budget, although there is some room for manoeuvre in the autumn pre-budget report. This creates a time lag in decision-making for fiscal policy, added to which there is an implementation lag because many tax changes cannot begin until the start of the new fiscal year in April, sometimes 1 or 2 years ahead. This means that if the government tries to respond to current economic problems using fiscal policy, the effect will not become apparent until the economy has started to change tack in the normal course of the economic cycle. Furthermore, when a government deliberately sets out to expand its spending, people will try to cash in on this by increasing their pay demands, and the effect will be increased wages and costs rather than expanded output.

Also, there are *crowding-out effects* of increased spending by governments. For example, if the government decides to build a new hospital, there is less scope for a private hospital in the vicinity providing essentially the same service. There is also crowding-out in the sense that when the government runs a deficit it needs to raise finance which, in times when credit is less readily available, stifles private initiative. However, it can be argued that expansionary fiscal policy simply causes inflation because the debt issued to finance the expansion, often Treasury bills, is so liquid that it acts like printing money.

> **Exam tip**
>
> If you are very sophisticated in your economics you will realise that when demand-side policies are contractionary, AD does not fall but rather rises more slowly. This could be shown by a smaller right shift in AD than was expected (you would need to show two shifts to show the relative changes). This advanced approach would earn you credit in the exam, but can cause confusion if you are still feeling unsure of your grasp of macroeconomics. Ask your teacher which approach you should use.

Links and common themes

There are many other critiques of fiscal policy and these are explored in Theme 4.

Supply-side policies

Supply-side policies include any action by the government intended to increase the amount that firms are willing to supply at any given price level. They involve improving the supply side of the economy, i.e. productivity, availability of resources, tax or benefit incentives, removing regulations that add to costs or other cost reductions. In other words, they seek to shift the AS curve to the right (Figure 11).

> **Knowledge check 31**
>
> If interest rate changes are not working, what else can be done to achieve economic objectives?

> **Exam tip**
>
> Make sure you know how changes in demand-side policies shift the AD curve. If fiscal policy is expansionary (e.g. a cut in tax or a rise in government spending), then shift AD to the right. If monetary policy is expansionary (e.g. a cut in interest rates or increased amounts of QE), then you also shift AD to the right.

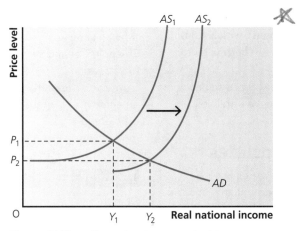

Figure 11 The effect of an increase in *AS*

Market-based and interventionist policies

There are two fundamental approaches to supply-side policies — that of increasing the effectiveness of markets (allowing more flexibility as determined by supply and demand) and the interventionist approach (governments getting involved in markets to reduce market deficiencies). As with demand-side policies, there are strong views as to which approach is more effective.

Market-based methods

- *Increasing price flexibility and signalling in a market*. If prices are not used to allocate resources effectively, there will be surpluses or deficits in the market. Imagine the government failed to increase the real rate of the minimum wage. This means that real wages would fall and there would be less unemployment in the labour market. Firms' real costs of production would therefore go down and the *AS* curve would shift to the right.
- *Increasing competition*. Reducing artificial constraints such as legal monopoly rights, as in the UK Royal Mail, can increase competition. As firms compete, they must either cut costs or become more innovative in order to survive, which effectively shifts the *AS* curve to the right by reducing costs. Another way to increase competition is to privatise, although there is little scope left for privatisation of publicly owned firms in the UK. **Deregulation** is another option — this happened in the 1980s in the UK with the freeing up of the bus and coach sector.
- *Improving incentives*. Incentives function by giving people higher rewards for what they do and therefore motivating them to work harder. The most obvious way to do this is to cut marginal income tax rates or reduce corporation tax, which is a tax on a firm's profits.

Interventionist methods

- *Improving education and training*. This could be anything from increasing spending on pre-school education to offering firms subsidies to take on apprentices. Clearly, these approaches are expensive and there can be huge time lags.
- *Improving health and introducing performance-related pay*. These are longer-term policies that encourage firms to produce more at any given price level.

Knowledge check 32

Are supply-side policies likely to have an impact on fiscal policy? Does this mean that they are the same thing?

Deregulation The process of reducing government rules and restrictions on businesses.

- *Implementing regulation.* A recent example is the Financial Stability Board (which, like the MPC, is chaired by the Governor of the Bank of England), which stops banks from taking high levels of risk or encouraging consumers to borrow more than they can manage.
- *Improving* infrastructure. A new runway at Heathrow could be argued to be a supply-side policy because it will reduce costs for firms in terms of unreliable communications. Similarly, HS2 could reduce travel time by train.

Strengths and weaknesses of supply-side policies

Although some supply-side policies are clearly very effective — for example, deregulation in the phone industry has resulted in greatly improved standards in terms of price levels and aftercare service — there are some industries in which there is either no opportunity for increased competition or where the benefits are outweighed by increased costs. For example, many believe that increased competition in the NHS has merely resulted in increased management costs rather than improved efficiency.

Another issue with supply-side policies is the time lag. Some policies, most notably in education, can take many years to have any effect on production costs. If anything, in the short run they increase costs because there are fewer people in the labour market.

One of the strongest arguments against supply-side policies is that if there is demand-deficient unemployment then the supply-side policies could have no effect at all. Japan is often used as an example, where for over 25 years there has been an increase in productive capacity but a real deficiency in demand and no change in equilibrium unemployment. This can be illustrated by shifting the *AS* to the right but the *AD* crosses on the horizontal part of the *AS* curve. The equilibrium point does not move, even though the *AS* has shifted out (Figure 12).

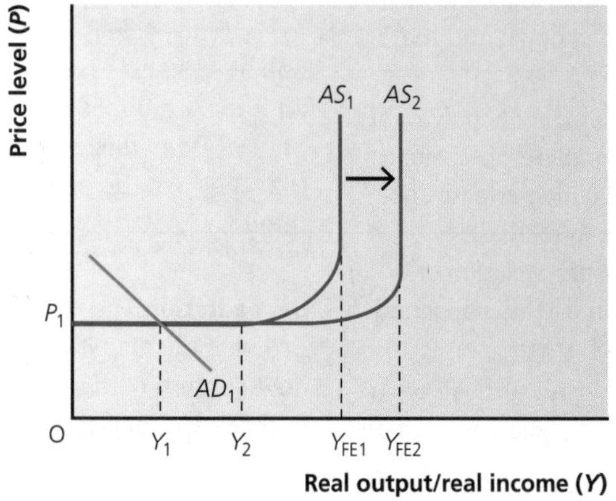

Figure 12 A rightward shift in the long-run *AS*

Supply-side policies can cause poverty and inequality. The policy to cut out-of-work benefits such as Jobseeker's Allowance might indeed encourage some people to find a job, but if there are no jobs available or the skills do not match then the result will be no effect on the labour market and a wider income distribution. The same is true of cuts in the national minimum wage and the policy of reducing the power of the trade unions.

Infrastructure
The physical and organisational framework needed for an economy to operate efficiently.

Exam tip
Remember that many interventionist policies are expensive and could cause conflicts with the demand-side policy approach.

Knowledge check 33
Are changes in interest rates supply-side policies?

Trade unions
Organisations of workers that exist to promote the welfare of their members.

In addition, supply-side policies have side effects on the demand side. For example, cutting taxes has fiscal policy implications. Perhaps the most important aspect is that cutting minimum real wages and reducing trade union power affects lower income earners adversely and disproportionately. However, effective supply-side policies do have the benign outcome of both lower inflation and higher rates of economic growth.

Useful exercises

Read the minutes of the latest MPC meeting at the Bank of England website (www.bankofengland.co.uk). Go to 'Monetary policy', then 'MPC minutes'. List eight factors that the MPC has taken into account in making its interest rate decision, showing in each case how these relate to the price level in the UK.

Links and common themes

In taking this subject further in Theme 4, you will gain a more international perspective on these issues.

Exam tip

Supply-side policies can have a benign effect, in that they increase output at the same time as reducing pressure on prices.

Knowledge check 34

What would be the result of successful supply-side policies if there were a significant amount of spare capacity in the economy?

Summary

- Demand-side policies are used to shift the *AD* curve. They include monetary and fiscal policies.
- Supply-side policies are used to increase the *AS* in an economy. They involve measures that are often microeconomic in effect, in that they aim to influence individuals and firms to become more productive, cutting costs, improving incentives and increasing competitiveness, thereby being able to produce more at lower prices.
- Most governments use a combination of both demand-side and supply-side policies to stabilise prices and maintain growth rates in the economy.

Conflicts and trade-offs between objectives and policies

In this section a limited range of conflicts has been chosen, although for each objective there are issues with every other objective. Some objectives, such as growth and employment, have more in common than others, such as inflation and the environment. The degree to which there is conflict is a useful way to approach your evaluation.

Inflation and unemployment

Consider this scenario. You are running a nightclub and the DJ is asking you for a wage increase. She may be good at the job, but you are not keen to pay more for the same service because it will eat into your profits. What do you do? If there were a whole selection of unemployed DJs eager and willing to take up the post, you would probably look to employ a replacement at the same or possibly at a lower rate than your current DJ. However, if DJs are in short supply and the success of your club depends on having a good DJ whom you can rely on, you would be more likely to enter into discussion with your current DJ to keep her on board.

In other words, a shortage of labour in a specific field can cause wage pressures to build up. The net effect in the wider economy is that, as wages go up, people start spending more, the costs of production increase because labour is a major production cost and inflation begins to rise. In other words, low unemployment or reduced spare capacity leads to higher inflation.

This basic analysis is the rationale for the short-run **Phillips curve**, which was an observation of an apparent **trade-off** between unemployment and inflation (measured by the rate of change in wages) in the UK between 1861 and 1913 (Figure 13).

Phillips curve An observation of a trade-off between unemployment and inflation.

Trade-off When one factor can only improve at the expense of another.

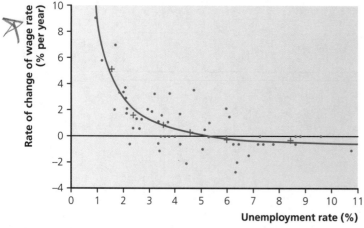

Figure 13 The relationship between inflation and employment in the UK, 1861–1913

Source: 'The relationship between unemployment and the rate of change of money wages, 1861–1957', *Economica* (1958)

In practice, if a government starts trying to exploit this trade-off it is unlikely to have the desired result. For example, because of the transparency of a government's actions, if it tries to spend its way into reducing unemployment the most likely effect

Exam tip

Although most students can draw and label a Phillips curve, few can explain *why* inflation falls when unemployment rises, and vice versa. Even fewer can evaluate the concept.

will be an increase in wages to absorb the government's extra spending, i.e. inflation. As inflation goes up, newly employed workers will soon realise that their wages are being eroded by inflation and firms will realise that they are not getting as much profit out of their workers because of inflation. Therefore, any increase in employment is not likely to last in the long term. For these reasons, although the Phillips curve is an observable phenomenon, it is not necessarily a viable tool for government.

Exam tip

The Phillips curve is often called 'short run' because many economists believe that if you put any pressure on the trade-off relationship (e.g. trying to engineer lower unemployment by allowing a little more inflation), the trade-off breaks down. In other words, the long-run Phillips curve is vertical. You do not need to know this for your exam, but it is useful to know that not everyone takes the same view of the Phillips curve.

Economic growth and the balance of payments on the current account

As an economy grows and incomes rise, consumers are likely to demand more imports. Firms' incentives to export will diminish as it is easier to find eager customers in the domestic market. Therefore, economic growth is likely to worsen the current account. The main exception to this is export-led growth (see p. 39). A second reason why growth might not necessarily worsen the balance of payments is if the growth is caused by an increase in AS. For example, owing to decreases in costs or increases in investment, an economy will become more internationally competitive, meaning that the economy can export more and import less while growing.

Increased employment and the sustainable environment

If more workers are employed, there is likely to be more congestion on the roads and more carbon use because of more offices, more manufacture and greater energy usage. In addition, as people's incomes increase, workers are more likely to go abroad for their holidays and most foreign travel involves increased carbon emissions.

On the other hand, higher employment can mean that the government has more scope for taxation and one spin-off might be the opportunity to use 'green' taxes — where taxation is specifically designed to reduce carbon use. For example, road tax has been increased for 'gas-guzzling' vehicles. The effect of higher employment also depends on whether the increase is in the manufacturing or service sector. As more people can work remotely in the service sector, it may be that an increase in employment has a negligible effect on the environment.

Economic growth and income redistribution

When an economy grows, incomes are most likely to rise at the top end of the income spectrum such as in the form of bonuses for sales executives. The effect is a widening of income inequality. However, over time, people at the high income end of the scale

Exam tip

The Phillips curve can be used to show that there is a trade-off between the objectives of low unemployment and low inflation.

Knowledge check 35

If the government wants to cut unemployment, it might find that the level of wage inflation starts to rise which might cause inflation more widely. Explain why this is.

Knowledge check 36

Consider the effects of economic growth on the environment. Make a list of points to show why they conflict and then evaluate each point.

may employ people from lower income groups such as domestic staff. Increased demand for low-skilled labour should eventually lead to increased wages.

Nevertheless, many critics argue that, although there may be some transferred benefits of growth, there is a two-track labour market and those with low skills rarely benefit because, as skill shortages develop, immigration fills the gaps and the wages of low-skilled workers do not rise. Another counter-argument is that, even if wages rise by a constant percentage for everyone, income inequality still increases in absolute terms.

Inflation and equilibrium on the balance of payments

Low inflation should help to improve a balance of payments deficit on the current account. Low prices relative to other countries mean that exports become more attractive on world markets and imports are less attractive. However, if the balance of payments tends to be in surplus, control of inflation does not restore equilibrium in the sense of removing a surplus.

Furthermore, when one of the main objectives of macroeconomic policy is to control inflation, interest rates might be tighter than they would be otherwise. High interest rates often mean that the exchange rate rises: 'hot money' flows in as funds move between international capital markets seeking the best interest and exchange rates. A strong currency makes a country's exports less competitive and its imports relatively cheap, worsening the trade position in the long run as demand for exports and imports responds to the price changes.

Links and common themes

There is a link with the externalities analysis in Theme 1 and the role of the state in Theme 4.

Summary

- The Phillips curve is an empirical observation that there is a negative correlation between inflation (i.e. wage inflation) and unemployment.
- The Phillips curve is used by some to argue that there is a trade-off between unemployment and inflation and that if an economy can tolerate increased inflation then there would be lower long-term unemployment.

- Trade-offs can also be seen to exist between the other government macroeconomic objectives.

Knowledge check 37

Why does relatively low inflation improve the balance of payments on the current account?

Knowledge check 38

Can you sketch a Phillips curve?

Have demand-side and supply-side policies worked?

In the years before the last UK recession of 2008–09, the UK saw economic growth at a trend of between 2% and 3% per annum for 15 years, and inflation hardly reaching 3%. However, in 2008 growth became negative in the wake of the credit crisis and inflation was persistently above the ceiling of the inflation zone for several years after that. Since 2014 CPI has been below the 2% target and fell significantly below the 1% floor in 2015.

Unemployment as measured by the Labour Force Survey rose markedly after the credit crunch as the recession sank in — from 1.6 million at the start of 2008 to around 2.5 million in 2011 — but it has since fallen to below 2 million.

The trade in goods of the balance of payments recorded a £46 billion deficit, just over 5% of GDP, while the current account deficit as a whole was £46 billion (3% of GDP) at the height of the boom in 2007. The pound has fallen 25% against the euro since 2008, which is by far the most important trading currency for the UK, and has lessened the deficit. Since then the pound has recovered around a quarter of its fall, meaning that exporting is less easy, but there is much less pressure on inflation (a weak pound makes imports expensive, which causes cost-push inflation). However, remember that in the short run a fall in the value of a currency tends to worsen the current account because the price elasticity of demand for imports and exports is almost zero.

The distribution of income is described on the Office for National Statistics website (go to www.ons.gov.uk then type 'Gini' into the search box), where you can see the effects of taxes and benefits on household income. This cutting of the Gini coefficient demonstrates how governments can directly change the level of inequality.

Perhaps the least achieved government objective is the protection of the environment. Clear and unambiguous indications are given in national statistics on carbon emissions. The Kyoto Protocol, ratified by 170 countries (excluding the USA), expired in 2012 with no significant reduction in carbon emissions or other greenhouse gases. A new protocol is in place aiming for a level 18% below the 1990 levels of carbon emissions but, without the USA's backing, this agreement too may fail to be significant on a worldwide level. Although the UK has seen some improvement, it fell far short of its target. The EU Emissions Trading Scheme, which was set up in 2005, has yet to lead to carbon reduction, but if the prices of permits rise (fewer are issued) this situation should improve. A new ETS since 2012 has included the aviation industry and reduces the number of permits available.

Although each of these objectives can have serious effects on economic agents if it is out of control, some clearly have a more immediate impact on people's lives. For example, unemployment not only means lost income, it can also mean a long-term reduction in a person's employability through loss of skills and training. However, it might be that the government cannot solve unemployment in the short term. Many economists believe that too much cushioning of the unemployed results in an inefficient labour market, and that competition and increased incentives for those out of work are a better approach to dealing with unemployment.

Similarly, inflation of 2% is not thought to be a problem, and as long as incomes move in line with inflation there will be no serious side effects. Most people's wages, as well as student grants and pensions, are adjusted in line with inflation, so reducing inflation below this level is not a priority. However, as inflation rises there comes a point where it erodes international competitiveness, discourages foreign inward investment and causes income redistribution away from savers to borrowers to such a degree that its destabilising effects become a major concern.

A current account deficit on the balance of payments is of no concern to governments if there is enough trust in the capital markets and the value of the currency. It is, however, a sign that the country may be overspending relative to its income and at some point the outflow of money will have to be compensated by inflows. The UK has international investments abroad with enormous earning potential, which may mean that the balance will be restored if the situation is left to itself (laissez faire). Therefore, many economists think that the UK government should not try to rectify a current account deficit with demand management. However, most agree that supply-side policies should be used to restore competitiveness in the long run.

Perhaps the most contentious of policy objectives is the idea of taxing the rich and giving to the poor. Social spending by the UK government on income support accounts for about one-third of government expenditure: five times the amount spent on defence. Many would argue that redistributing income from the rich to the poor through taxes and benefits is simply unfair, destroys incentives and reduces the work ethic. The main drawback with social expenditure is that it has little effect on reducing poverty; some argue that it can even create a 'dependency culture'. Although this might be true in general, extreme poverty is debilitating and leaves potential workers caught in a cycle of worklessness. They may be unable to sustain permanent employment at the available rates of pay because of personal circumstances, a need to care for dependants, a lack of skills or the high cost of housing.

Useful exercises

- Look at the UK fact sheets available at the Economic and Social Research Council website at www.esrc.ac.uk. Follow the 'Resources' link and there are many thought-provoking articles about the impact of government policies. There are pages on productivity and distribution of wealth, to name just two.
- To see a breakdown of government spending, go to the Office for Budget Responsibility website. Look up the latest budget or read a guide on public finances such as the one at http://budgetresponsibility.org.uk/brief-guide-public-finances-2. Look at the final page showing where taxpayers' money is spent. These objectives are revisited in more depth when considering the role of the state in Theme 4.

Summary

- The priority given to the seven macroeconomic objectives depends on the political stance of any particular government.
- The aim of government is often not to reach a zero rate of, say, unemployment or inflation, as this would cause increased pressures elsewhere in the economy. It usually seeks a balance between the objectives.
- The government does not itself finance a deficit on the balance of payments. A deficit could, however, cause a fall in the UK banking system's reserves of foreign currency and result in a downward movement in the value of the currency — it is only in this respect that the government aims to maintain a balance, if at all.

Do macroeconomic policies conflict?

Fiscal policy and supply-side policy

Increased government spending may be used as part of a fiscal policy to increase AD, and much of this spending will be directed to the health and education sectors. In this case, fiscal and supply-side policies are working in tandem to improve growth prospects and the supply-side effects may cancel out any ill effects on the price level from the expansion in demand.

By contrast, if a government is using contractionary fiscal policy as a means of trying to control the price level, the impact might be a leftward shift of the AS curve. Therefore, prices might rise rather than fall and output might contract even further than intended.

Fiscal policy and monetary policy

Although fiscal and monetary policies are both demand-side policies, if a government runs a budget deficit this has to be financed, which will affect the money markets. Much of the budget deficit is financed by issuing government 3-month Treasury bills, which offer investors secure and liquid assets that are easy to trade on the money markets. This helps with stability during a credit crunch, but at other times it might be inflationary because it increases liquidity available. A looser fiscal policy can mean that the MPC favours a tighter monetary policy, taking into account the **fiscal stance** in deciding whether to raise interest rates.

Monetary policy and supply-side policy

A tight monetary policy means that interest rates are higher than they perhaps need to be. Although this may control inflation, it increases costs for firms if they are borrowing money. By contrast, raising interest rates tends to make exchange rates rise. As UK firms import nearly all their raw materials, the effect on production costs may be significant. Therefore, tight monetary policy can instead improve the supply side, although higher exchange rates are not guaranteed and they harm firms trying to export. In the case of cutting interest rates, as in loose monetary policy, this can reduce borrowing costs for domestic firms. However, if the exchange rate falls, firms will face increased import costs but gain competitiveness internationally.

Useful exercises

- Look in the *Financial Times* for the prices of Treasury bills. Note that they do not earn interest; instead they are issued at a discount on their redemption price. Choose a bond and work out what the interest is by working out the discount on the time left before it is redeemed and then calculating this as an annual figure.
- Visit the Institute for Fiscal Studies website at www.ifs.org.uk where you can get access to a simulation model of the whole economy. You can then be your own Chancellor, put in extra public spending, track the change in national income over time and see the multiplier at work.

Knowledge check 40

What are macroeconomic policies?

Knowledge check 41

What is contractionary fiscal policy?

Fiscal stance The position that the government takes on fiscal policy.

Exam tip

Many answers confuse the impact of a change in the interest rate on the exchange rate. Usually they move in the same direction.

Knowledge check 42

If the government wants to borrow heavily, how does this affect the distribution of income?

Content Guidance

Links and common themes

You do not need an in-depth understanding of money markets, but there are links with the way shares work (Theme 1) and with the significance of public sector borrowing (Theme 4).

Summary

- There are three macroeconomic policies that you need to know. On the demand side there are fiscal and monetary policies; on the supply side there are the supply-side policies. There are other macroeconomic policies when looking at economic development, but you do not need to know them for Theme 2.
- Some analysts doubt that expansionary fiscal policy has any positive effects at all. If the long-run *AS* curve (*LRAS*) is vertical, only inflation would occur.
- Monetary policy is clearly powerful in controlling *AD*, but it is a blunt tool and can have damaging effects on income distribution and across the supply side of the economy.
- Supply-side policies are now rather limited in their potential in the UK and interventionist policies can cost a great deal for the government in terms of fiscal policy. However, policies aimed at increasing investment in the economy can have benefits in the future despite fiscal implications in the short run.
- A fiscal deficit means that the government needs to borrow from the money markets. This can produce two very different side effects, depending on the type of credit available in the money markets. If there is a shortage of long-term funds, there may be crowding-out as the government can offer good terms and security. However, if the money is lacking liquidity and the government borrows short term, issuing Treasury bills is a little like printing more money. This effectively loosens the money markets, which can be inflationary.

Questions & Answers

Exam format

AS exam Paper 2, 'The UK economy: performance and policies', comprises 50% of the weighting for the AS examination. The paper comprises two sections: section A consists of five multiple-choice and short-answer questions; section B consists of one data-response question broken down into a number of parts including a choice from an open-response question.

The time allowed for the examination is 1 hour and 30 minutes. There are a maximum of 80 marks: 20 marks are available in section A (the multiple-choice and short-answer questions) and 60 marks in section B (the data-response question) of the exam paper. This means around 25 minutes should be spent on section A and 60 minutes on section B, leaving 5 minutes to check and amend your work.

A level Paper 2, 'The national and global economy', comprises 35% of the weighting for the A level examination. The paper comprises three sections: section A consists of five multiple-choice and short-answer questions; section B consists of one data-response question broken down into a number of parts; section C consists of a choice of extended open-response questions.

The time allowed for the examination is 2 hours. There are a maximum of 100 marks: 25 marks are available in section A (the multiple-choice and short-answer questions), 50 marks in section B (the data-response question) and 25 marks in section C (the extended open-response question). This means around 25 minutes should be spent on section A, 60 minutes on section B and another 25 minutes on section C, leaving 10 minutes to check and amend your work.

Practice paper 1: AS

Section A

Section A questions are fairly straightforward and the danger is in writing too much or spending too much time on this section. You might expect to be given data on one of the four measures of economic performance and the skill will be measured in how carefully you interpret the data.

Answer ALL questions. Use the data to support your answers where relevant. You may annotate and include diagrams in your answers.

Question 1

The table below shows CPI levels in 2014 in the UK.

Month	CPI level
February	127.4
March	127.7
April	128.1
May	128.0
June	128.3
July	127.8

Source: ONS

(a) Explain the term 'deflation'. (1 mark)

ⓔ There is only 1 mark, so just ensure the explanation is fully accurate. Don't go beyond a definition.

(b) Calculate the inflation rate for the 6 months up to and including July 2014. You are advised to show your working. (2 marks)

ⓔ Give the formula and show your working. Remember to take a calculator to the exam.

(c) Which one of the following can be inferred from the table? (1 mark)

   A Food prices were higher in July 2014 than in February 2014

   B There was deflation between June 2014 and July 2014

   C Prices were rising at a constant rate over the period shown

   D Interest rates will rise

ⓔ Again, just 1 mark for multiple-choice questions. Ensure you look out for the 'distracter', which is trying to steer you away from the correct answer.

Student answer

(a) Deflation is when the general level of prices falls. It differs from disinflation, which is a rise but more slowly than they have been rising in the past. This happened between April and May 2014 in the period shown. Prices fell by just 0.1 index points. This might be good for people with savings because their spending power will rise.

ⓔ 1/1 marks awarded. Clearly for just 1 mark this is far too much. The answer has strayed into parts of the questions which appear later on the paper.

(b) The rate of inflation is Change / Original value × 100, so:

$$\frac{127.8 - 127.4}{127.8} \times 100$$

$$= \frac{0.4}{127.8} \times 100$$

$$= 0.31\%$$

ⓔ 1/2 marks awarded. This is a common mistake. Although the formula given is correct, the data for the original value is in fact the final figure. Even top further maths students make mistakes such as this.

(c) B

ⓔ 1/1 marks awarded. This is the observation that was made by the student in part (a), but at that point there was no available credit. Note that A is a very effective 'distracter' because we know that the general level of prices had risen, but we cannot say what had happen to food without any more information. If you look at the data from the ONS, you could see that food prices had fallen over this period.

ⓔ Total score for Question 1: 3/4 marks.

Question 2

In 2013 the Bank of England estimated the marginal propensity to save by UK households as shown in Figure 1.

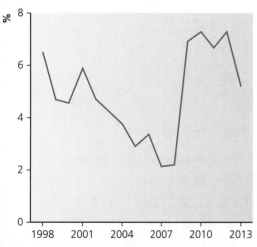

Figure 1 Household saving ratio

Source: ONS and Bank calculations

(a) Explain the term 'marginal propensity to save'. (1 mark)

ⓔ Note that the question shows a percentage for the savings ratio, but the question is about marginal propensity to save which is usually given as a ratio of between 0 and 1. Don't let this alarm you — answers as percentages or ratios are equally acceptable.

(b) It is estimated that the value of the other withdrawals apart from saving add up to 0.8. Calculate the value of the multiplier for the UK in 2014. You are advised to show your working. (2 marks)

ⓔ This is a new area of the specification and to find practice questions you will have to search more widely than recent Edexcel past papers. Good textbooks should provide a range of examples.

(c) Which one of the following is a likely implication of this value of an economy's multiplier when there is an initial injection from outside the system? There will be: (1 mark)

A An increase in the rate of unemployment

B An improvement on the balance of payments as imports rise

C A larger effect on GNP than on GDP

D A larger effect on total output than the initial injection

ⓔ This question requires a straightforward definition of the multiplier.

Student answer

(a) The marginal propensity to save is the proportion that is saved from any extra amount that is earned.

ⓔ 1/1 marks awarded. This is clearly understood.

(b) The multiplier is:

$$\frac{1}{(1 - 0.2)}$$

$$= \frac{1}{0.8}$$

$$= 1.25$$

ⓔ 2/2 marks awarded. This answer gives the formula and a correct calculation. Nothing more is required for full marks.

(c) D

ⓔ 1/1 marks awarded. If correctly calculated in part (b), the multiplier of 5 would have a large magnifying effect on an injection. However, if part (b) is answered incorrectly it is still possible to get this question correct.

ⓔ Total score for Question 2: 4/4 marks.

Question 3

The following data show the forecast government taxation and spending for the year 2014–15.

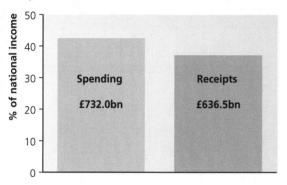

Figure 2 Government taxation and spending, 2014–15

Source: ONS and Bank calculations

(a) What will be the fiscal position for the financial year 2014–15 according to these estimates? (1 mark)

A There will be a balance of payments deficit of £95.5bn

B There will be a balance of payments surplus of £96.5bn

C There will be a budget deficit of £95.5bn

D There will be a budget surplus of £96.5bn

ⓔ Never confuse the fiscal position ($G + T$, the government's own record on spending and tax) with the balance of payments ($X - M$).

(b) Give one reason for the fiscal position shown. Use your own knowledge of the UK economy in recent years to explain your answer. (3 marks)

ⓔ Only 3 marks are available and 1 mark is for simply stating the point. It could be the state of the economy cycle, structural problems, the financial crisis or government decision to use expansionary fiscal policy. Remember that you only need to give one answer.

Student answer

(a) C

ⓔ **1/1 marks awarded.** This is correct — and it also 'feels' correct. You can probably rule out all the answers with 'surplus' in before you start.

(b) The government has a large fiscal deficit because there has been a major recession. In a recession the amount the government receives from taxes falls because there are fewer people working paying less tax and there are more people who are receiving out-of-work benefits such as Jobseeker's Allowance.

ⓔ **3/3 marks awarded.** This is an efficient answer, with clear use of terms and helpful application of the tax and benefit changes.

ⓔ **Total score for Question 3: 4/4 marks.**

Question 4

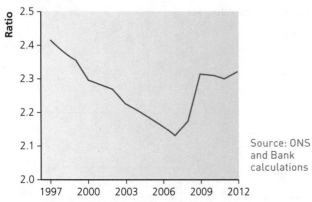

Figure 3 UK capital stock as a proportion of GDP

(a) Explain the term 'investment'. (1 mark)

ⓔ Remember not to confuse investment with anything to do with buying shares or saving. These are the most common problems with explaining this term.

(b) Distinguish between gross investment and net investment. (1 mark)

ⓔ This is a new part of the syllabus and the key concept you need to use is depreciation.

(c) Give one reason for the change in the trend in the investment ratio shown in Figure 3. (2 marks)

ⓔ Remember to identify the trend before you start the answer. Also ensure you know the date of the financial crisis. Don't say anything that is counter-intuitive such as 'business confidence rose in 2008 as a result of the crash'.

Student answer

(a) Investment is an increase in the capital stock.

ⓔ **1/1 marks awarded.** This answer is short but absolutely correct.

(b) Gross investment is an increase in assets in total spending terms, whereas net investment takes into account wear and tear on the assets and the fact many capital goods become out of date quickly.

ⓔ **1/1 marks awarded.** Again, this answer is accurate.

(c) The recession hit the UK economy in 2008 after the financial crisis had kicked it off in the autumn of 2007. Investment is determined by many things apart from GDP, and did not fall as quickly as GDP. GDP shrunk significantly in the period after 2008, so even if investment did not change, investment as a proportion of GDP would have risen as GDP fell.

ⓔ 2/2 marks awarded. Figure 3 is a hard graph to interpret because the figures on investment per se are not as one might expect — falling before the crash and rising afterwards. This candidate has done extremely well to look carefully at the data and answer with a valid response.

ⓔ Total score for Question 4: 4/4 marks.

Question 5

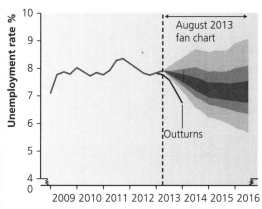

Figure 4 The probability of various outcomes for Labour Force Survey employment

(a) Explain the term 'unemployment'. (1 mark)

ⓔ This needs to be precise. Remember that you need to have the concept of the LFS in your answer.

(b) Figure 4 shows projections for LFS employment. Calculate the change in unemployment from the third quarter of 2011 to the expected level for the end of 2013. (2 marks)

ⓔ You will not be able to measure this exactly from the graph, but there is a generous margin of error in the marking as long as you get the calculations right.

(c) Which one of the following statements is correct? The change in unemployment means that: (1 mark)

　　A Employment is rising

　　B The aggregate demand curve will shift to the left

　　C The long-run aggregate supply curve has shifted to the right

　　D The number of Jobseeker's Allowance payments will probably decrease

ⓔ Remember that the values for unemployment and employment do not add up to 1 and depend on activity rates. Unemployment might be falling because more people are becoming inactive (not in fact the case) or because the workforce is shrinking (e.g. because of emigration).

Student answer

(a) Unemployment is the number of people who would like to work but cannot currently find a job.

ⓔ 0/1 marks awarded. There are many people without paid work but many, such as students, are not classified as unemployed. Remember to refer to the labour force or the economically active.

> **(b)** 8.2 – 6.7 = 1.5
>
> $$\frac{1.5}{8.2} \times 100$$
>
> = 18.3%

ⓔ 2/2 marks awarded. The correct formula is used and the data are handled correctly.

> **(c)** D

ⓔ 1/1 marks awarded. A correct response, showing the link between unemployment and the fiscal position.

ⓔ Total score for Question 5: 3/4 marks. Total score for Section A: 18/20 marks.

Section B

Study Figures 5, 6 and 7 before answering Question 6. Answer ALL Questions 6 (a) to (e) and EITHER Question 6 (f) OR Question 6 (g).

Question 6 The UK's aggregate supply: relative productivity, oil and commodity prices

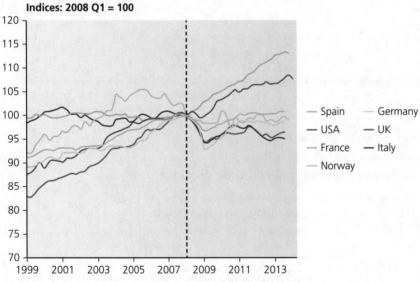

Figure 5 Labour productivity per head in selected countries

Source: Eurostat, ONS, Thomson Reuters Datastream and Bank calculations

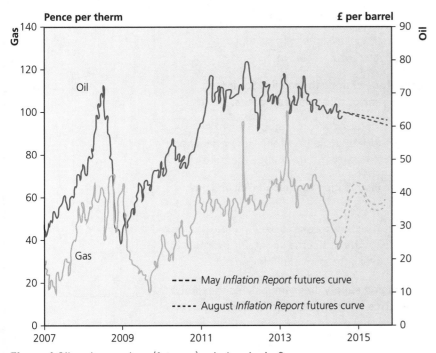

Figure 6 Oil and gas prices (futures), wholesale, in £

Source: Bank of England, Bloomberg, Thomson Reuters Datastream and Bank calculations

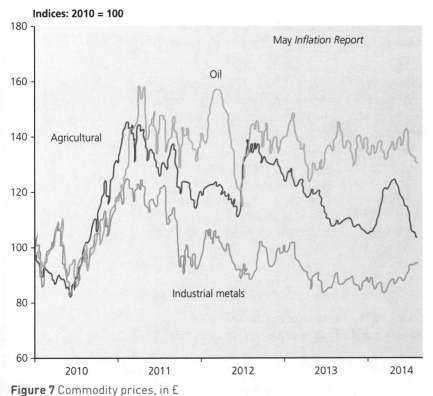

Figure 7 Commodity prices, in £

Source: Bloomberg, S&P Indices and Thomson Reuters Datastream

(a) Refer to Figure 5. Explain what is meant by the term 'productivity gap'. (4 marks)

ⓔ Productivity is a measure of how efficiently resources are used, i.e. output relative to inputs. Don't confuse it with production.

(b) Using Figure 6, calculate the percentage change in the oil price index between 2012 and 2014. Use start of year or mid-year estimates. (5 marks)

ⓔ The question requires you to read the scales accurately and perform a percentage change calculation. It is important to avoid using the wrong scale and to remember what is the *original* figure for the percentage change formula.

(c) Explain the likely impact on UK income distribution when foods, oil and gas prices rise. (6 marks)

ⓔ For income distribution questions, you must identify groups of people and how they are affected in terms of the proportion of their income spent, for example, on food. There are 2 marks for knowledge, 2 for application and 2 for analysis.

(d) With the aid of an aggregate demand and supply diagram, assess the likely impact on the UK's real output and price level of the trend in oil prices over the period shown. (10 marks)

ⓔ Oil prices affect aggregate demand through *X* and *M* (the UK is a net importer) and through *AS* because oil is a major production cost. Remember that for 'assess' questions (10 marks), you have to evaluate.

(e) Apart from food and oil prices, discuss two factors that the Bank of England's Monetary Policy Committee considers when it makes its interest rate decision. (15 marks)

ⓔ Factors could include house prices, wages and productivity — but the list is enormous. Avoid 'soft' arguments such as those saying that the MPC considers current interest rates or inflation when making its decision. It is a weak argument to say that you look at inflation to explain what is going to happen to inflation. If you look at the current situation and can make inferences from it — for example, by observing a trend — this would be a valid argument, but on its own it is not convincing to the examiner. Similarly, saying that you look at interest rates to decide what is going to happen to inflation is like saying someone looks at how strong their sun cream is to see what the weather will be. Sun cream is used to prevent the adverse effects of the weather; in the same way, the interest rate is used to prevent the worst repercussions of inflation. There are much easier ways to approach this question by looking at the *causes* of inflation (such as wage pressures). Remember again that you have to evaluate for 15-mark questions.

EITHER:

(f) Using an appropriate diagram, evaluate the likely effect of the change in productivity on the level of aggregate supply and the price level in a country such as the UK. (20 marks)

(e) Although it looks daunting, the 20 marks for the essay can be broken down into clearly defined sections that can be used for all the essays you will encounter. Knowledge (such as definitions) is worth 4 marks; application of the data provided and your own knowledge are worth 4 marks; analysis of the processes involved such as transmissions mechanisms or the use of diagrams are worth 6 marks; and evaluation is worth 6 marks. Make two or three analysis and evaluation points for each.

In all macroeconomics papers, the diagram expected will almost always be an *AD/AS* diagram and a shift to the right in *AS* would be an improvement in productivity. Don't forget to mark on the changes in equilibrium points and to use a large arrow to show the shift.

OR:

(g) **Evaluate the benefits and costs of growth for a country such as the UK, using the information provided.**   (20 marks)

(e) For this part there are 4 marks for knowledge and understanding, 4 marks for the application of the concept, 6 marks for analysis that shows the processes involved and 6 marks for evaluation, making a total of 20 marks. Remember to use the Levels of Response reproduced in all mark schemes to see exactly how the marks are applied.

For this essay, choose at least one benefit and one cost. Don't write out a full list of costs and benefits, but develop your points as fully as you can using the data provided.

Student answer

(a) The difference in output per unit of input between various countries. **a** It includes manufacturing and construction. It ignores productivity in areas such as farming (primary) and services (tertiary). **b**

(e) **3/4 marks awarded.** **a** Definition questions must always be brief but precise. Productivity must be distinguished from production by looking at factor inputs as well as outputs, so use of the phrase 'per unit of input' makes this a good answer. **b** Data reference would be advised in any question that refers you to a source. Choose a country and quote the figures relative to the UK, e.g. Italy has 2% lower productivity than the UK.

(b) Using mid-year estimates:
$$\frac{57 - 62}{57} \times 100 = -8.77\%$$

(e) **5/5 marks awarded.** This student has selected the correct years, read the data accurately from the graph and used the correct formula of Change / Original value × 100. Remember to include the minus sign if it is a fall.

(c) Everybody needs food and rich people probably spend more on food than poor people, so I would guess that income distribution doesn't change much, if it improves at all. 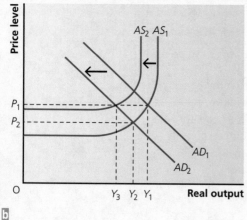ª However, it depends which food gets more expensive. If it's fast food, it might affect poor people more, but if it's caviar it would affect rich people more.

ⓔ 2/6 marks awarded. ª It would be wise to mention the proportion of income spent, not the absolute values. Rising food prices mean that lower income groups have less money to spend after food has been paid for. However, the gross income remains unaffected unless you want to argue that rising food prices somehow reduce the gross income of lower income groups; it would be better to argue in the evaluation that the income distribution changes *after* food costs have been taken into account.

From the brevity of the answer it is clear that this student is on unsure ground. If you are uncertain, it is unwise to tell the examiner you are guessing; instead, follow through your ideas with reasons as far as you can. This is not an evaluative question. The candidate wastes time in attempting to evaluate.

(d) The UK is a net importer of food and oil. Although we produce both, we buy more in value terms from abroad than we export. When prices of these commodities go up, the response by consumers is very small — in other words, there is low price elasticity of demand. When *PED* is less than 1, a rise in prices means that total expenditure rises, so when the prices of these goods go up, total expenditure on imports rises. Imports are a negative component of *AD* (aggregate demand) and therefore *AD* falls. This effect is made more extreme by the multiplier effect. ª

ᵇ

The increase in commodity prices also affects aggregate supply (*AS*), which in a sense is the cost of production. All producers need oil and food in the UK and therefore all firms' costs will rise, so *AS* shifts to the left, prices rise and output falls.

Overall, the price effects might outweigh each other but the output effects will reinforce each other (return to P_1), and we would expect a fall or a slowdown in real output Y_3.

ⓔ 10/10 marks awarded. This answer includes ⓐ the multiplier and ⓑ an accurate diagram, and covers both the *AD* and *AS* sides of the case. Most answers will give only the *AS* side and this one stands out as far better than the average. Evaluation is required and is worth 4 marks. These are earned by showing that the forces outweigh or reinforce each other.

(e) First factor: The MPC takes into account the current account of the balance of payments. If there is a deficit such as the one the UK is currently experiencing (£45 billion), this is a sign that the UK economy is spending more than it is selling abroad, and it might be that the pound will fall in the future, which is inflationary (imports become more expensive). However, the deficit itself is not inflationary and therefore the MPC is unlikely to be worried directly by a deficit. In fact, if *X – M* is less than zero, there is a negative effect on *AD*, which reduces inflationary pressure.

Second factor: The MPC looks carefully at house prices. If house prices are falling, as they were during the autumn of 2007, this can mean that there is a negative wealth effect. ⓐ In the USA this triggered a credit crunch and interest rates have had to fall dramatically to try to keep demand up. ⓑ If demand is falling, there will be unemployment. ⓒ

ⓔ 11/15 marks awarded. The first paragraph is an ideal answer. The current account is one of the many thousands of factors looked at by the MPC when making its interest rate decision. A deficit may mean that inflation will not hit the target. The answer stresses the role of the MPC and the inflation target and gives real-world evidence.

Turning to the second factor, ⓐ wealth effects are the effects on spending (or similar) when asset values change. ⓑ Interest rates are cut to stimulate spending and investment in an economy. ⓒ However, there may be a time lag. Unemployment is a lagging indicator, meaning that it tends to worsen after the worst of a recession is over.

This student adopts a common approach to this type of question and starts off well. By focusing on some real data and the concept of wealth effects, the answer hits on an important area of concern for the MPC. But then no link is made to inflation — instead, the answer heads off to talk about unemployment, which may well be an important consideration for the government but is of no direct concern to the MPC.

(f) Increased productivity lowers the costs of production for firms because they can produce more output for the same factor costs. Aggregate supply increases and price levels should fall. 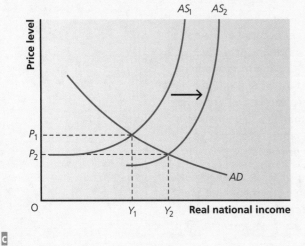 This is because the UK has seen recent rises in relative productivity. b

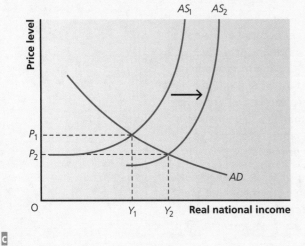

c

🟢 **14/20 marks awarded.** a The shift is described correctly and the word 'costs' is used, which is crucial for AS questions (4 marks). b There is an attempt to apply the concept to the UK and to use the evidence provided in Figure 5 (2 marks). c 4 marks are earned for a fully labelled diagram. It shows the new and old price level — a detail that the examiner will be looking for. In cases such as this where the question is fully addressed, full marks will be given for KAA despite the brevity of the response. The 6 marks available for evaluation are *not* awarded.

🟢 **Total score for Section B: 45/60 marks.**

(g) One benefit of growth is that incomes are rising, and if incomes are rising, people are likely to have higher standards of living. Economic growth is one of the seven macroeconomic objectives of governments, and growth has two main causes. The causes of growth a are a shift to the right in the *AD* and a shift to the right in the *AS*. *AD* might rise because consumption, investment, government spending or exports have risen or because saving, taxes or imports have fallen. There is a multiplier effect. *AS* might rise because there is a fall in investment, a fall in production costs such as wages or a rise in the exchange rate making imports cheaper.

The benefits of growth b for consumers are that they can buy more goods and services with their higher incomes or they could have longer holidays and shorter working hours. Benefits for the government are that it receives higher tax revenue (this assumes that the tax thresholds remain the same) and this means that it is easier for the government to make income distribution more equal by the 'Robin Hood' process of taxing the rich to give to the poor. Firms also benefit because they have higher profits (because they sell more) and even the environment might improve because rich countries that have signed the Kyoto Protocol of 1997 are committed to using cleaner and greener methods of production. These methods cost money, which the increased income from the growth can pay for through an increase in tax revenues.

The costs of growth are the environmental damage. More production means more pollution and depletion of natural resources. Also, income distribution might not get better because it tends to be the rich people who get richer quicker when the economy is growing, whereas people like cleaners get paid the same. Higher incomes usually involve longer workings hours, not shorter ones.

ⓔ 10/20 marks awarded. ⓐ This student has made a classic error in starting with the *causes* rather than the *effects* of growth. Although this does not lose this student any marks, nor does it gain any, and there is an opportunity cost in that less time can be devoted to relevant material.

ⓑ The student has listed the standard points for and against the benefits and costs of growth, but the evaluation is limited. It is clear from the answer that there are two sides to every point, but it would be better to discuss the advantages and disadvantages of each point in turn and then come to a reasoned conclusion.

An important evaluation point that could be made is that the effects might be different in the short run and the long run. For example, although economic growth often makes income distribution worse in the short run, these incomes might even out over time as the 'rich' spend their money, with multiplier effects. A second evaluation point might be that the effect on the environment might be difficult to measure and it depends on whether the growth is based in the industrial or services sector. In the latter case, the environmental aspects may not be so significant.

To summarise, this student would score well on analysis marks but is lacking application (4) and evaluation (6).

ⓔ Total score for Section B: 42/60 marks.

Remember that *either* (f) or (g) is awarded, and here both have been attempted. The examiner in this case marks both questions, and the higher scoring essay is awarded. This is not a recommended approach for a student: it is far better to choose one essay and do it really well.

Practice paper 2: A level

Section A

Section A questions are fairly straightforward and the danger is in writing too much or spending too much time on this section. You might expect to be given data on one of the four measures of economic performance and the skill will be measured in how carefully you interpret the data.

Answer ALL questions. Use the data to support your answers where relevant. You may annotate and include diagrams in your answers.

Question 1

The graph below shows changes in employment in the UK since 2010.

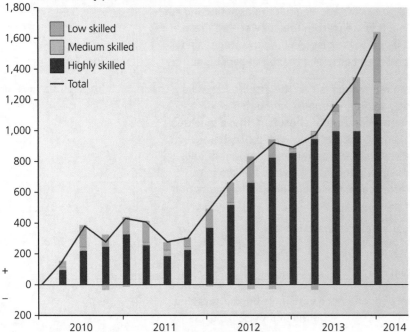

Figure 1 Employment changes in the UK, by occupational skill level

Source: Labour Force Survey and Bank calculations

(a) Calculate the change in employment over the period shown. (2 marks)

ⓔ There is 1 mark available for data selection and 1 mark for applying the concept of 'cumulative'. Be careful to read the axes correctly.

(b) Explain one possible reason for the changes in the types of employment. (2 marks)

ⓔ There are many possible answers. Just make sure that the reason you give supports the data you choose.

(c) Which one of the following can be inferred from the graph?   (1 mark)

    A   The inactivity rate has fallen

    B   The level of unemployment has fallen

    C   There has been a decrease in underemployment

    D   The number of employees has risen

ⓔ Again, just 1 mark available for multiple-choice questions. Ensure you look out for the 'distracter', which is trying to steer you away from the correct answer.

Student answer

(a) 600

ⓔ **0/2 marks awarded.** Read the axes carefully — the correct answer is 600,000. Then use the concept of cumulative, that is, increasing by successive additions.

(b) The biggest rise was in low-skilled workers, in terms of percentages. This rose because there has been a rise in consumption and many workers are required in retail jobs.

ⓔ **1/2 marks awarded.** This is a valid reason, but the student should say *why* consumption rose. Was the recession over? Would a calculation help?

(c) D

ⓔ **1/1 marks awarded.** The distracters make you think about the other parts of the specification and in practising these you should think about why the other options are incorrect.

ⓔ **Total score for Question 1: 2/5 marks.**

Question 2

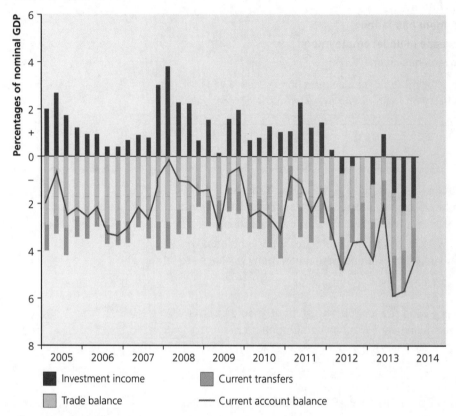

Figure 2 The UK current account

Source: *Inflation Report*, August 2014, Bank of England

(a) Explain the term 'the current account of the balance of payments'. (1 mark)

ⓔ Be careful to think beyond *X* and *M*.

(b) Explain the trend in the current account in the period 2013–14. (2 marks)

ⓔ Try to give two pieces of data for a 2-mark question.

(c) Which one of the following is a likely reason for the current account position over the whole period shown? There has been: (1 mark)

   A   An increase in the rate of unemployment

   B   An improvement on the balance of payments as imports rise

   C   An increase in the rate of UK productivity

   D   A tendency for the UK to run a trade in goods deficit

ⓔ This is a straightforward question on a deficit in the UK.

(d) **Give one reason why the UK current account might improve in the near future.** (1 mark)

ⓔ Be careful to make reference to the UK. You cannot refer to a manipulation in the rate of the pound, for example, or the imposition of tariffs.

Student answer

(a) The current account balance is a record of the difference between inflows and outflows between countries. It includes trade in goods, services, investment income and current transfers.

ⓔ **1/1 marks awarded.** This is clearly understood.

(b) The deficit worsened then improved towards the end of the period.

ⓔ **1/2 marks awarded.** This answer gives the correct trend, but there needs to be some use of the actual numbers for the second of the 2 marks.

(c) D

ⓔ **1/1 marks awarded.** An accurate response.

(d) This is because the UK doesn't make anything any more.

ⓔ **0/1 marks awarded.** The trade in goods is always a deficit in the UK because we have a comparative advantage in services (you will cover the concept of comparative advantage in Theme 4). However, this explanation is weak in that it does not use any theory, just some journalese that is incorrect (the UK makes cars, whisky, cashmere etc.).

ⓔ **Total score for Question 2: 3/5 marks.**

Question 3

The following graph shows the forecast government taxation for the year 2014–15.

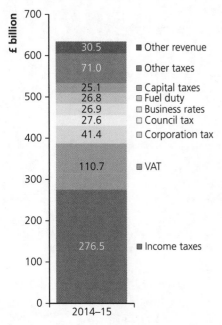

Figure 3 Sources of public sector (government) revenues

Source: Office for Budget Responsibility

(a) What can be inferred from the graph? (1 mark)

A The single main source of government revenue is from indirect taxation

B The single main area of government spending is direct taxation

C Indirect tax contributes more to government income than tax on firms' profits

D There will be a budget deficit of £95.5bn

ⓔ You need to understand direct and indirect taxes, and know what they mean.

(b) Which of the tax revenues shown in the graph are likely to rise in a boom or recovery phase of the trade cycle? Use your own knowledge of the UK economy in recent years to explain your answer. (3 marks)

ⓔ You might talk about more workers, earning more (income tax), firms making more profit (corporation tax), more consumers spending more (VAT) or the government's decision to use expansionary fiscal policy.

(c) Suggest one possible trade-off with other government policies if the rate of tax imposed on fuel duty is decreased. (1 mark)

ⓔ The question is clearly looking for a trade-off with environmental objectives, but there are others such as inequality that you could use.

Student answer

(a) C

ⓔ **1/1 marks awarded.** This is correct, but don't be tempted to add up all the individual tax revenues.

(b) The government has more revenue from workers, firms and spending. The graph doesn't show how much this has changed.

ⓔ **1/3 marks awarded.** This is an efficient answer in terms of identification, but there is no reason why these tax revenues change and no use of recent UK knowledge.

(c) There is likely to be more petrol use because people will not be deterred from driving or flying because of the high marginal cost of extra fuel. This means more carbon emissions, which is proven to damage the ozone layer and cause global warming.

ⓔ **1/1 marks awarded.** There is no need to write a whole essay on global warming for a 1-mark question.

ⓔ **Total score for Question 3: 3/5 marks.**

Question 4

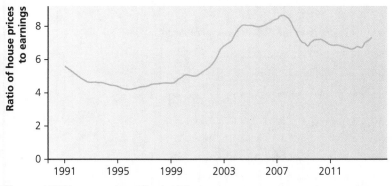

Figure 4 UK house price affordability

Source: ONS and Bank calculations

(a) **Using the graph provided, explain what has happened to house price affordability in the UK.** (2 marks)

ⓔ The trick is to pick out the part of the data that is relevant.

(b) Which of the following is the likely relationship between house prices and
house price affordability? When house prices rise: (1 mark)

A Houses are more affordable

B People tend to take out larger mortgages relative to their incomes

C Incomes fall

D People tend to find it harder to withdraw equity from their houses

ⓔ This question involves many concepts that confuse students and it is worth
discussing what it is like to have a mortgage with someone you know.

(c) Explain the likely impact of a rise in house price affordability on the level of
aggregate demand. (2 marks)

ⓔ If houses are more affordable, this may mean there is more confidence in the
economy and *AD* might increase. However, rising house price affordability might
mean that house prices in many cases are falling, so you could also argue for a
fall in *AD* because of negative wealth effects. Either response is credited as long
as the point is justified.

> **Student answer**
>
> **(a)** House prices are becoming less affordable, but not as much as before the
> 2008 crash. This means that the ratio of house prices to incomes is higher
> and this can be seen in the graph. The average house price is now seven
> times average income, which is a high and dangerous figure, showing that
> house prices are difficult to afford.

ⓔ **2/2 marks awarded.** This is clear, absolutely correct, and makes appropriate
use of the data.

> **(b)** B

ⓔ **1/1 marks awarded.** Again, an accurate response.

> **(c)** This means that the ratio of house prices to incomes is higher and this can
> be seen in the graph. The average house price is now seven times average
> income, which is a high and dangerous figure, showing that house prices
> are difficult to afford. This might mean there is a crash in house prices in
> the future, as some people cannot afford to pay their mortgages and default
> on their loans. This would mean *AD* falls. But it might not be the case
> because the animal spirits might make prices rise even more.

ⓔ **2/2 marks awarded.** The answer repeats part of (a), showing it would be
advisable for students to look at all parts of the question before they proceed.
However, this candidate has done well to look carefully at the data and answers
the question with a valid response.

ⓔ **Total score for Question 4: 5/5 marks.**

Question 5

The MPC's central projection in the May Report, under the assumptions that Bank Rate followed a path implied by market interest rates and that the stock of purchased assets remained at £375 billion, was that four-quarter GDP growth would ease slightly in the near term, but that it would remain relatively steady thereafter. Inflation was expected to be at, or slightly below, the target throughout the forecast period. The MPC judged that there was scope to make further inroads into slack before an increase in Bank Rate was necessary.

Source: *Inflation Report*, May 2014, Bank of England

(a) Explain the term 'quantitative easing'. (2 marks)

ⓔ This definition should go far beyond the idea of 'printing money'. QE is a major part of monetary policy and needs to be explained carefully.

(b) Explain the likely effects of a reduction in the stock of purchased assets of £375 billion. (2 marks)

ⓔ The process described is called 'tapering' and it is likely to ease monetary tightness.

(c) Which one of the following statements is correct? The raising of interest rates is likely to reduce the level of: (1 mark)

A Inflation

B Unemployment

C Surplus on the balance of payments

D Inequality

ⓔ Data can be presented in verbal as well as numerical form, as given here.

Student answer

(a) QE is when the government prints money to stimulate the economy.

ⓔ **0/2 marks awarded.** There is little here to show that the student has studied economics more than just reading the tabloids.

(b) Prices will rise and inflation will be stimulated. This is just as if the interest rates had been cut.

ⓔ **0/2 marks awarded.** The candidate has not read the question carefully. The question is about QE in reverse — the tapering back of the asset purchase scheme. This will have the same sort of effect as raising interest rates.

(c) A

ⓔ **1/1 marks awarded.** A correct response, showing a basic understanding of monetary policy.

ⓔ **Total score for Question 5: 1/5 marks. Total score for Section A: 14/25 marks.**

Section B

Read Extracts 1 and 2 before answering Question 6.

Question 6 Conflicts between fiscal policy and other government policy

We expect tax receipts to rise much faster than spending over the next 5 years, so we forecast that the deficit will get smaller each year. Indeed, by 2018–19 we expect the Government to be running a small surplus on current policy, at which point receipts would be slightly above 38 per cent of national income and spending slightly below.

Swings into deficit have become steadily more pronounced over the post-war period. And budget surpluses have been achieved in only 12 years since 1948.

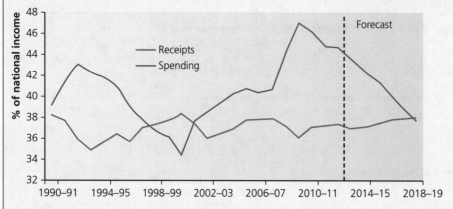

Figure 5 The gap between government receipts and spending

Source: ONS

We expect the current deficit to be £67.6 billion in 2014–15 and there to be a current surplus of £30.5 billion in 2018–19.

One of the Government's fiscal targets is to achieve balance or surplus on the structural current budget balance at the end of each five-year forecast horizon, thereby borrowing only to finance investment, which is presumed to deliver a lasting flow of benefits over time. We expect that target to be met by a big margin of £31.3 billion in 2018–19, which was the target year in the 2014 Budget forecast. We also expect a modest surplus in 2017–18.

The main rate of corporation tax fell to 20% in 2015, from 26% in 2011. Oil and gas prices fell dramatically over the year, meaning that corporation tax revenues for the government were significantly reduced to £2.8 billion from £10 billion a year in recent years, but overall tax revenues are expected to grow by 24% over the next 5 years.

Source: Office for Budget Responsibility

Extract 2 Using the Budget to make it easy to go green

Friends of the Earth, which is calling on the Chancellor to deliver on his promise to put sustainability at the heart of his forthcoming Budget, has produced a blueprint for a green Budget. It outlines a variety of measures the government must adopt to help the UK to develop a low-carbon economy, including a windfall tax on energy and a £10 billion tax shift programme raising taxes on pollution and cutting taxes on income, jobs and people.

Friends of the Earth's Economics Co-ordinator Simon Bullock said: 'Carbon dioxide emissions just keep on rising. We've had enough of half measures and green spin. The Chancellor must put climate change at the heart of the Budget and make it cheaper and easier for people to go green.'

Source: Friends of the Earth

(a) Explain what is meant by the term 'fiscal policy'. (5 marks)

ⓔ Apart from referring to spending (G) and taxation (T), you must use the data and put fiscal policy in the context of the government's budget.

(b) With reference to Extract 1, using an appropriate diagram examine how the cut in tax on firms' profits outlined in the extract may be used to promote growth without inflation. (8 marks)

ⓔ Cutting taxes on firms is a supply-side policy aimed at shifting *AS* to the right, although in other contexts it can be fiscal policy.

(c) Assess the likely impact on the distribution of income in the UK which will result from the changes to fiscal policy described in Extract 2. (10 marks)

ⓔ For income distribution questions, you must identify groups that are affected such as employees and students on fixed incomes.

(d) With reference to Extracts 1 and 2, discuss ways in which fiscal policy may be used to incorporate environmental goals. (12 marks)

ⓔ Governments can use both spending patterns and appropriate taxes in order to change the way consumers and firms have an impact on the environment. For example, they can cut taxes on greener fuels or subsidise the installation of solar energy-generating equipment.

(e) Evaluate the likely effect of changes in fiscal policy for the decisions on monetary policy made by the Monetary Policy Committee. Consider both the short run and the long run in your response. (15 marks)

ⓔ When a government operates a loose fiscal policy, the shortfall in tax revenue has to be found by raising funds in the money markets. This demand for funds puts an upward pressure on interest rates but in the long run, if the fiscal policy is effective in creating jobs and encouraging growth, the effects on monetary policy could be reversed.

Student answer

(a) Fiscal policy is the government's manipulation of its spending (G) and taxation (T) in order to affect aggregate demand. Fiscal policy decisions are made by the government in the budget in March, although some further changes are often made in the autumn pre-budget report. Fiscal policy can be used to achieve a variety of policy objectives, mainly economic growth, employment and the distribution of income. Increasingly, in the views of some economists, fiscal policy has included 'green taxes' as a means to prevent further environmental problems.

If government spending is increased relative to taxation, fiscal policy is said to be expansionary and AD shifts to the right. If government spending is increased at a slower rate than taxation, fiscal policy is said to be contractionary. a We expect the current deficit to be £67.6 billion in 2014–15 and there to be a current surplus of £30.5 billion in 2018–19.

ⓔ **5/5 marks awarded.** a Accurate answers such as this earn full marks including data marks.

(b) Cutting taxes in the economy implies that the government is aiming to increase output and spending. This can be shown by a movement to the right of AD on the real output axis. We expect tax receipts to rise much faster than spending over the next 5 years, so we forecast that the deficit will get smaller each year. Price levels will increase and output will increase. There will be a multiplier effect, which is the knock-on effect when an injection such as G increases while T stays constant.

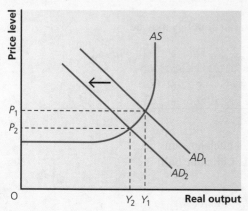

There will also be an impact on the supply side of the economy. If people are paying less tax, there will be an incentive to work harder for those already in work, and those who are not in the workforce (the economically inactive) will have an increased incentive to join the workforce. As the workforce increases, wages will be bid downwards and the economy becomes more competitive. a However, there is not likely to be much change in the short run, as profit taxes will not have much impact on firms if demand is so low that they are not making significant profit, and the change in profit tax might be too small to have much effect. The falls in aggregate demand thanks to cuts in the public sector and cuts in benefits will more than likely outweigh any increases in supply that result from the cuts in taxes because firms are unlikely to increase investment in a time of economic uncertainty.

🄔 **6/8 marks awarded.** The analysis is weak because on the demand side there is not likely to be a significant increase — there are several cuts in *G* that more than outweigh any fall in *T*. Just because the government is cutting expenditure, you cannot assume that taxes will rise or even fall. The supply side is considered well. The shift in *AD* is not correctly applied in the diagram because the answer says *AD* increases but the diagram shows it decreasing. It would also be better to incorporate both shifts on one diagram to show the overall effects on output, with both of the shifts increasing the equilibrium real output. Therefore, full marks are not earned for the diagram; this student receives only 1/2 marks available. 🄐 The student receives 2/2 marks for evaluation, awarded as 1 + 1 for considering magnitude issues and outweighing factors. Alternatively, one argument could have been developed more fully for 2 marks.

(c) In general, a tax windfall like this is likely to help lower income groups by a larger proportion than higher income groups. Therefore, the distribution of income will 'improve' in the sense that inequalities are reduced. However, this masks some of the picture.

In Extract 2 it is stated that there is a windfall tax on energy and a £10 billion tax shift programme raising taxes on pollution and cutting taxes on income, jobs and people. Shifting the burden of tax is intended to have environmental impacts, but there will clearly also be an effect on the distribution of income. Although the tax changes will affect the distribution of income (when taxes are cut on lower income groups and raised on large profitable firms that are causing pollution), it is not made clear which income taxes are being changed from the data provided. For example, if it is the top rate of tax (45% on incomes above £150,000 in the UK) it will widen the gap between income groups. Furthermore, at the other end of the income distribution people who don't have any work at all will not gain from a fall in income tax and again the distribution of income will widen. Another evaluation point to note is that global warming affects the poorest people across the world, and so in taking a global view the use of 'green' taxes will reduce the gap between the rich multinational companies and the poor producers in developing countries.

🄔 **10/10 marks awarded.** The analysis is secure because two groups are identified and the relative change in income for these groups is described. The evaluation is also highly awarded (4/4) because the student pulls out inadequacy in the data. Other ways to evaluate would be to say that the increased government borrowing will have to be paid back at some point and it is not clear which part of the population will pay that. In addition, other things are not equal. Lower income taxes might attract more investment from abroad, which might mean more job opportunities for people in the UK. More demand for workers will make wages rise.

(d) Green taxes can be used as part of fiscal policy. This is where the main aim of the policy is not to change *AD* but to change the way in which spending occurs so that carbon dioxide emissions are reduced. One obvious way to do this is to increase the tax on petrol. Of course no one likes paying more, but the net effect on consumer disposable income need not change overall because the government could spend more on public services such as transport. In Extract 2 this is called a '£10 billion tax shift programme' and the emphasis is on changing the way in which taxes are imposed and not the overall tax burden. a

In my view, the cost of petrol is already far too high, b and most of the journeys that are made are necessary to the way our economy works. In other words, demand is price inelastic because the public services are totally rubbish. c Trains are overcrowded and buses only go along the main, congested routes and never at times to suit demand. If the private sector was running the transport system it might not be any better, but I cannot see how throwing money at the public sector is going to help. You cannot have more trains running on the Underground; it's already at full capacity. Transport is the main thing stifling productivity growth in the UK and green taxes are not going to help.

e **9/12 marks awarded.** a The good thing about this answer is that it uses the extract, describes how green taxes would work and goes on to evaluate. b The bad thing is that the comments are rather over-enthusiastic in rhetoric and measured analysis is the opportunity cost here. c Rather than using words such as 'rubbish' and 'of course', more effort could be put into offering a viable solution and other forms of evaluation.

(e) The MPC considers an enormous range of data when coming to a decision on the interest rate. It looks at pressures in the labour market, the housing market, commodity prices, external exchange and the global economy, to name but a few. The fiscal stance is also of great interest to the MPC. If the government is seen as operating a loose fiscal policy as outlined in Extract 1, the MPC might consider the impact on the real side of the economy and on the money markets. Government spending has to be financed and if it is not going to be financed by taxation then the money has to come from somewhere, in this case by borrowing. It is the extent to which borrowing affects inflationary pressures which is of concern to the MPC. The MPC has only one objective: to maintain the inflation target. Therefore any softness by the government in its fiscal policy is likely to be compensated for by tight monetary policy, i.e. a raising of interest rates.

The borrowing can have two very different effects on inflationary pressures. If there is spare capacity in the economy, expansionary fiscal policy can cause some increased growth without damaging inflationary pressures. If there is no spare capacity — i.e. full employment — then there will be inflation. This can be shown using an *AS* curve and, as the elasticity falls (the *AS* curve gets steeper), the inflationary pressures increase. a

There is a similar set of opposites in the money markets. If there is plenty of credit around, extra government borrowing will not have much effect on the cost of credit. But in times of the 'credit crunch' when it is hard to get loans and interbank loans are at high interest rates, increased borrowing will crowd-out the market. In this case, government expansion will not be inflationary and will merely tighten the monetary side of the economy.

In conclusion, it is difficult to say how the MPC will react to expansionary fiscal policy. It depends entirely on the context. If there is spare capacity in the economy and there is plenty of available credit, it is unlikely to react. But in the case where bottlenecks are appearing and prices are edging upwards, the MPC might raise rates. If the money market is short of credit, however, this might not be needed as increased cost of credit will in itself control aggregate demand and therefore restrain inflationary pressures.

ⓔ **14/15 marks awarded.** This is a sophisticated response on what is probably the most challenging part of the specification. ⓐ The only noticeable weakness is the absence of a diagram, although the shape of the *AS* curve is described well. A simple sketch to illustrate the bottlenecks in supply would earn 2/2 diagram marks rather than the 1 mark earned from describing it.

ⓔ **Total score for Section B: 44/50 marks.**

Section C

Answer ONE question from this section.

Question 7

Discuss the likely effects on the price level in the UK if interest rates are raised. Consider the impact on the economy of a change in the exchange rate in your answer.

(25 marks)

ⓔ This is a question about tight monetary policy, i.e. raising interest rates. The aim is to decrease inflationary pressures by suppressing aggregate demand. The transmission mechanisms by which interest rate changes impact upon *AD* include changes in consumption and investment and changes to net trade. The effect on net trade may occur because the exchange rate changes. Remember that changes in the interest rate and the exchange rate tend to happen in the same direction — if the interest rate rises, so does the exchange rate.

Student answer

If interest rates are raised there will be an impact on most of the components of aggregate demand, $C + I + G + (X - M)$. First we look at consumption (C). C falls for many reasons. One is that savings become more attractive and loans become more expensive. People will be less inclined to take money out of savings to spend and will be less inclined to borrow if they have a choice about their spending. For example, someone might choose to delay buying a car. People will find things bought on hire purchase will have higher monthly instalments, so they will be less inclined to borrow in this way. Also C falls because mortgage interest payments will increase so people will have less money left over to buy goods and services. People may feel less confident about the economy so they might rein back their spending plans. This would be especially true for people who have their own businesses and expect sales to fall.

Investment (I) will also fall when interest rates rise. This is because the interest rate is the cost of borrowing money for investment and only very profitable projects will be worth taking the risk of investing in when interest rates are too high.

$X - M$ will be likely to fall. This is for two reasons. The first is that we will export less (as firms face higher interest rates there are increased production costs) and imports will fall (we will suck in fewer imports because our spending is down). The second reason is that the pound is likely to rise. This is because 'hot money' will be attracted to the pound as sterling bank accounts will be earning higher returns. With a strong pound imports are cheap and exports are dear (SPICED). This means that M will rise and X will fall, so AD will fall. This is made even more pronounced because of the multiplier. AD falls meaning prices will fall and output will fall. [a]

The extent of the impact on the price levels depends on where on the AS curve the AD crosses. If AS is very inelastic (the steep part), the impact on the price level will be very large. The economy will have very little spare capacity and there will be strong pressures to increase prices. A rise in the interest rate will relieve much of the pressure on prices as people stop spending and the price level will fall significantly. However, if the AD crosses the more elastic part of the AS curve, there will be little effect on prices and a large effect on the level of output and probably employment in the country. Raising interest rates will just bring more gloom in an economy where there is a lot of spare capacity already and people deciding to spend less will cause further stagnation in the economy. [b]

Another evaluation point is that the interest rate impact does not always happen immediately. Many people have fixed rate mortgages and, even if mortgage interest payments do change, the mortgage holder might not react straight away. It is the same with the exchange rate. Even if the pound gets stronger, it probably won't make people stop buying things from the UK. If foreign tourists have booked their holidays already, they won't cancel if the pound gets stronger. They might just think more carefully about where they go in the future. This is a time lag, and it depends on the price elasticity of demand for exports and imports. [c]

ⓔ **23/25 marks awarded.** An excellent analysis (16/16 marks). ⓐ There are just a couple of points to note on the analysis side: the SPICED acronym is really useful for you to remember the effect of a change in the exchange rate, but you don't need to tell the examiner about it. The first point about $(X - M)$, with X falling and M rising due to changes in spending in the UK, is really a repeat of the argument about C, so it would have been better just to do the analysis concerning the change in the exchange rate, as indicated in the question.

The evaluation marks are ⓑ 5/5 and ⓒ 2/6. There is one good piece of evaluation followed by a slightly less developed attempt. The student might have offered a third point: for example, that the pound is influenced by many things apart from the interest rate or that relative interest rates are important, so the Fed and ECB rates need to be taken into account. Also in evaluation, if interest rates rise and AD slows, firms in the UK might look for new export markets to keep sales figures buoyant, so the balance of payments might not worsen as much. Then three pieces of evaluation could be rewarded 2 + 2 + 2 and full marks would be awarded overall.

ⓔ **Overall, despite some uncertain areas in the question as a whole, the student gets to an A by making sure that the longer answers pull up the grade.**

Question 8

To what extent is it likely that policies intended to increase economic growth will conflict with the working of other government policies? (25 marks)

ⓔ Remember that you only need to think of a maximum of three conflicts and should focus on policies not objectives.

Student answer

Policies intended to increase growth can be reflationary demand-side polices such as monetary and fiscal policy or supply-side policies. Fiscal policy might be used to increase aggregate demand by increasing government spending (G) or cutting taxation (T). Monetary policy can be used to increase growth by cutting interest rates, although in the UK the Monetary Policy Committee does not aim to increase growth — it rather allows growth to occur by cutting interest rates when inflation falls below target. These shift AD to the right and the effect on national income is magnified by the multiplier effect.

These policies are likely to conflict with the working of policies to improve the environment. Green taxes can be used to try to change the way people use goods and services with a high carbon use. Cutting taxes generally means that people have more money to drive large cars and fly to foreign countries for their holidays. The higher people's incomes become with economic growth, the less sensitive they are to green taxes. So even if cutting taxes in other areas outweighs the green taxes, the green taxes themselves will not have a very powerful environmental impact as the economy grows.

Supply-side policies are any action by the authorities to try to increase competition, incentives and the flexibility of the workforce. In the past they have included privatisation and deregulation, but they can also include tax cuts and legislation to reduce the power of the trade unions or cutting the national minimum wage. The aim is to shift the aggregate supply curve to the right. Costs will fall in the economy and the equilibrium will occur at a higher rate of GDP.

However, supply-side policies have side effects which might conflict with the workings of other government policies. For example, reducing the power of trade unions or cutting the national minimum wage is unlikely to improve the distribution of income. But in other ways the supply-side policies might improve the working of other policies such as monetary policy. As costs fall in the economy, this dampens inflationary pressures. Cutting taxes to improve incentives has a similar effect to expansionary fiscal policy.

🅮 **21/25 marks awarded.** This answer covers the main policies effectively and there are two good attempts at evaluation. The answer would gain full marks with the inclusion of a diagram showing how these policies affect price levels and real output or the equivalent written explanation. The 8 analysis marks and 4 application marks are most easily earned by applying the argument to an *AD/AS* diagram. There are three attempts at evaluation, but remember to give depth and breadth.

1 Increases in real GDP is the definition of growth.

2 Real values have the effects of inflation removed.

3 (For the purpose of your exam, you can treat GNI and GNP as the same thing.) GNI and GNP are different ways of measuring the same thing, i.e. the value or income/output of a country, including the net flows of income/output from production units abroad. Greece should certainly use GNI/GNP, a more reliable measure of living standards than GDP, because it gives a clearer picture of the extreme problems faced by its citizens.

4 Bhutan's happiness index takes account of the fact that in surveys people report being happy and not worried. Because everyone is equally poor, there is less anxiety about other people doing better among the residents.

5 Developing countries can grow more quickly because they are starting from a lower base, so the same input of £100m into a diamond refinery would have a larger percentage impact on growth figures in Botswana than in the UK.

6 An index is used to make comparisons over time and between countries. A base year is chosen and given the value 100, and changes are shown as percentage changes relative to the base year.

7 The expenditure survey shows us the proportion of income spent on each item, so that we can weight the price changes in terms of their importance to us as consumers. The price survey tells us the change in prices for each good and service that is bought.

8 No, they exclude the cost of mortgage interest repayments. There are not any measures of inflation which include the mortgage itself, because the mortgage debt does not change with inflation. If anything, mortgages decrease in real terms in times of inflation.

9 Housing costs are not included in the CPI measure used by many other countries. Housing costs include mortgage interest rates, which usually change when interest rates change, so raising interest rates (meant to reduce inflation) will in the short term make the rate of inflation higher if housing costs are included.

10 To do this it might help to know the deficiencies of each measure. For example, if you cannot claim Jobseeker's Allowance when you have a high level of savings, ILO unemployment will rise more quickly than the claimant count as people of all types, with various levels of savings, lose their jobs in a recession.

11 The focus of the answer should be on the two types of survey involved and there is opportunity cost involved in defining terms that are not required by the question. A weighted basket of goods, a price survey, an index and a base year should all form part of your answer.

12 In terms of the 'real economy' (actual goods and services), there are demand pressures (increases in *AD*) and cost pressures (decreases in *AS*). There is also the monetary effect of having too much money in the economy, chasing too few goods.

13 The current rate that the UK aims for is 2%, but other monetary authorities such as the European Central Bank view 2% as a ceiling and consider rates below 2% acceptable. Many economists think a little inflation is a good thing and most economists think high rates of inflation, say over 8–10%, are a major problem.

14 The employment level is the total number employed, whereas the employment rate is the total number employed relative to the number of people of working age.

15 The claimant count is the number of people who receive Jobseeker's Allowance. There are many who do not actually claim it for various reasons (they might not be out of work for long, for example). These people are not registered in the statistics for the unemployed, but they could be picked up by the ILO method.

16 The ILO records a wider range of ages and includes people who are not eligible to claim out-of-work benefits such as Jobseeker's Allowance. This may be because they have savings or their partner has a well-paid job.

17 New immigrants fill jobs that people in the UK either cannot or do not want to fill, increasing employment levels (but not necessarily employment rates). Some immigrants might displace UK workers, so UK workers might become unemployed. In addition, family members might accompany working immigrants in the hope of finding work and these people will eventually be able to claim unemployment status.

18 They are 'economically inactive' because they might be students, looking after dependants or carrying out other functions in the home.

19 Yes. The easiest way to decide whether or not something is an import is to look at the direction of the money flows. If money is leaving the country, the trade is an import.

20 It means that if the USA suffers a recession or a banking crisis, the effects will be felt more widely and deeply in the UK. This is because up to 17% of our exports go to the USA and our stock markets are inextricably linked, with many companies such as BP listed in both the UK and the USA.

21 No. People tend to consume about the same in total at lower prices, although they get more for their money. That is, *C* is roughly constant in money terms at various price levels.

22 It tends to rise because of the wealth effect.

23 No. If there is no spare capacity in the economy, the *AS* curve will be vertical, and Classical economists draw the *AS* curve as entirely vertical in the long-run situation. Keynesians draw the *AS* curve as a combination of horizontal (spare capacity), upward-sloping (some bottlenecks) and vertical (full capacity). Alternatively, for simplicity, you can draw a gently upward-sloping *AS* curve for the short run and a vertical or very steep *AS* curve for the long run.

24 A cut in education spending decreases *AD* (short term) and *AS* (long term).

25 A rise in interest rates cuts *AD* (short term) and *AS* (short-term increases in the cost of borrowing and long-term fall in investment).

26 An increase in productivity relative to the UK's main export markets leads to an increase in *AD* (as *X* rises and *M* falls, although only in the long term as price elasticity of demand is likely to be low in the short run) and a fall in *AS* if the relative cost of imports rises (short term) but an increase in *AS* if there is more investment from abroad (long term).

27 No. An increase in house prices tends to make people spend more, for two reasons. The first reason is that they feel more confident. The second is that they can take out loans using the increased value of their house as collateral, a process known as mortgage equity withdrawal.

28 No. The injections are investment, government spending and exports.

29 Actual economic growth is an increase in real GDP and potential economic growth is an increase in capacity in the economy.

30 This is not true if the increase is in potential growth and not necessarily true if the increase is in actual growth. It depends on the availability of spare resources, i.e. the output gap.

31 There are other aspects to monetary policy, such as quantitative easing. There are also fiscal policy and supply-side approaches to reach economic objectives.

32 Yes. Many supply-side policies have an impact on the fiscal position, but this does not mean they are policies aimed to shift *AD* and therefore we do not call them fiscal policies. The impact on the budget is a side effect.

33 Changes in interest rates are considered to be demand-side policies, but they do have supply-side impact. This is because the interest rate changes impact on the demand side more quickly and more significantly.

34 The result would be no change in output or the price level. A shift to the right in *AS* where *AD* crosses at the horizontal part of *AS* would have no impact on the economy except to increase the amount of spare capacity.

35 If there is a shortage of a particular type of worker, higher wages will need to be offered to attract workers from other jobs. As wages rise for some jobs and spending more generally increases, other wages and prices will be bid upwards.

36 ■ Economic growth can damage the environment because of industrialisation, e.g. pollution and congestion.

Evaluation: what about if the growth is in the service sector?

■ Depletion of natural resources.

Evaluation: more efficient use of resources.

■ Higher incomes mean more foreign travel, usually by air, increasing carbon emissions.

Evaluation: higher government revenues from taxation mean there is more money to clean up and introduce carbon-capping schemes or carbon offsetting.

37 It makes a country's exports relatively cheap and its imports relatively expensive. Remember, though, that the pattern of demand might not change immediately.

38

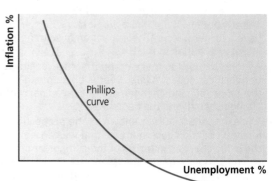

39 There are many arguments on both sides. Increasing benefits reduces poverty and inequality; or costs of living are rising so benefits should rise or the benefits will fall in real terms. Cutting benefits might make the unemployed more eager to get back to work as they cannot sustain living standards while out of work; or consider the opportunity cost of benefits; or consider the fiscal policy implications, e.g. taxes might have to rise, which might lead to disincentives in other parts of the labour market.

40 On the demand side, there are monetary and fiscal policies; on the supply side, there are supply-side policies. There are other macroeconomic policies, but you do not need to know them for A level.

41 Contractionary fiscal policy involves an increase in tax or a cut in government spending or both.

42 If heavy borrowing pushes up interest rates, this tends to affect lower income groups disproportionately more because lower income groups tend to have larger levels of debt relative to income.

Note: **Bold** page numbers indicate defined terms.

Index